TAX PLANNING FOR WOMEN

A STRATEGY TO PERMANENTLY REDUCE YOUR
TAXES AND BUILD WEALTH FASTER FOR EARLY
RETIREMENT

LISA CORBITT, CPA, MAFM

CONTENTS

FREE

1-HOUR TAX ASSESSMENT

We'll walk through...
-Which deductions you should be
taking.
-The legal entity structure most CPA's
don't recommend.
-The 2 retirement strategies even solid
financial advisors miss.

A Free Gift to Our Readers
Visit the link or QR code below to schedule your
FREE 1-hour tax assessment
www.amzaccountingsolutions.com/tax-planning-book

INTRODUCTION

66 "The hardest thing in the world to understand is the income tax."

— BY ALBERT EINSTEIN

Melissa is a self-employed entrepreneur and mom of two kids. She is passionate about her job and loves working for herself but often worries that she isn't saving enough for retirement. Between bills, debt, and regular expenses, it seems like each month, she is putting less and less away. When tax season rolls around, she experiences even more stress when faced with the complicated process of filing as a business owner. She knows that she can be doing more to get a better tax break but doesn't know where to start.

This book serves as a comprehensive guide to making the most of tax breaks and allowances for small business owners and entrepreneurs. It covers the basics of tax brackets, deductions, and credits before delving more specifically into the different strategies you can use to reduce taxable income and maximize returns. Written in a clear, easy-to-understand language, it's an accessible guide for the independent female entrepreneur.

Who Is the Author, Lisa Corbitt?

Lisa Corbitt is an established Certified Public Accountant. She is passionate about helping female entrepreneurs reach their financial goals with their small businesses. Having worked in the financial field for over 25 years, she is highly knowledgeable about taxes and how to work with your taxes to benefit you. Lisa is very passionate about building wealth and preparing for early retirement. She has experienced how an effective tax planning strategy makes someone's quality of life.

Many small business owners don't know how to maximize their savings within the first few years of operations. Many small business expenses could negatively impact the income that a business generates. Knowing how to leverage these expenses to work for you instead of against you is an acquired skill. With the guidance of this book, I hope to teach you about the expenses that you can use not only to save more but also to grow your small business.

As life hits us with a curveball, we need to pick it up and throw it back. Many tax benefits could potentially save you thousands of dollars when tax season rolls around. Owning your very own small business is challenging enough without worrying about your tax returns. You will learn what potential tax benefits you can leverage with the aid of your small business.

Investing in real estate could make a difference in the amount of income tax you are required to pay. Real estate not only generates an additional income for you but also provides you with beneficial tax incentives. These tax incentives are subject to change from year to year, so knowing what to look out for is very important. These incentives are presented to investors to motivate them to invest in more real estate properties and, by doing so increasing their income.

Another problem that small business owners are experiencing is the ability to save. Saving is a difficult concept for anyone to adopt as many individuals do not know where to start or what to do. The worry about saving for retirement or even unexpected expenses can take its toll on business owners. Knowing when to save and when to spend your profits is essential for any small business owner, and with the guidance of this manuscript, I intend for you to have a clear idea of the saving potential your business can have.

Investing in a few different assets could be a stressful experience but could significantly increase profits and reduce potential risk. Diversifying a portfolio works to your benefit because these assets react differently within the same economic event. There are a few things you can add to your portfolio to diversify it with the lowest risk possible. It is also your best protection against a potential financial crisis. You can learn to use a diversified portfolio to your advantage. All it takes is taking that first step.

Understanding the tax bracket you belong to is the first step to being able to change it. There are ways to decrease income and thus automatically move your tax bracket. In the following text, I will explain in more detail to teach you exactly how to change your tax bracket and save on your tax expenses.

Trying to figure out what tax credits and deductions mean can be confusing and frustrating, especially for a new business owner. I have compiled a comprehensive section within this book explaining both to help you understand what both mean for your business.

There is a lot of information on the internet regarding taxes, some extremely helpful and some useless. With this guide, you will find the most comprehensive information available. I have written this book intending to educate as many people as possible about everything tax related.

With the help and guidance of this book, you will learn and understand, amongst a few others, the following:

- Gain a deeper understanding of how taxes are calculated and applied and learn strategies to reduce tax rates.
- Feel confident in their ability to analyze your taxes and understand them, also effectively save for retirement.
- Discover the major deductions and credits available and how to claim them.
- Learn how to effectively reduce your tax bracket by

changing income streams and hiring family members/giving gifts.

- Find guidance on how to decide what entity type is right for your small business and what differentiates the types.
- Learn about the specific tax breaks available to small business owners and real estate investors.
- Learn about the four asset classes essential to strong strategic investing.

I hope you enjoy reading this book as much as I enjoyed putting it together for you!

1

TAX-FREE PLANNING–THE SECRET TO BUILDING WEALTH

I f you're reading this book, then it's a safe bet that you already know about the importance of tax planning. Tax planning is the analysis of your financial situation/plan to maximize tax breaks and minimize tax liabilities. In this chapter, I'll cover some important tax planning strategies and concepts that will be discussed in later chapters.

Understanding Your Tax Bracket

The United States operates under a progressive tax system, meaning that individuals with higher taxable earnings are subject to higher tax rates. There are seven federal income tax brackets: 10%, 12%, 22%, 24%, 32%, 35%, and 37%. The tax bracket you will fall under depends on your filing status and taxable income. A few other defining factors determine your tax bracket; these include adjustments, dependents, deductions, tax credits, etc. The tax system has been implemented to ensure that all taxpayers pay the same rates based on their income. Tax rates are calculated based on the highest amount of taxable income earned. Deductions, adjustments, and exemptions are not factored in when your bracket is determined. It only determines your income tax rates for additional income without rounding off the amount. A progressive tax system exists; therefore, we have federal tax brackets. As your income progressively increases, so does the tax rate that you are required to pay. Income tax brackets for 2022 are calculated according to the table below:

Rate	For Unmarried Individuals	For Married Individuals Filing Joint Returns	For Heads of Household
10%	$0 to $10,275	$0 to $20,550	$0 to $14,650
12%	$10,276 to $41,775	$20,551 to $83,550	$14,651 to $55,900
22%	$41,776 to $89,075	$83,551 to $178,150	$55,901 to $89,050
24%	$89,076 to $170,000	$178,151 to $340,100	$89,051 to $170,050
32%	$170,051 to $215,950	$340,101 to $431,900	$170,050 to $215,950
35%	$215,951 to $539,900	$431,901 to $647,850	$215,951 to $539,900
37%	$539,901 or more	$647,851 or more	$539,901 or more

Regardless of the tax bracket you fall into; you won't pay that rate on your entire income for two reasons:

- You can subtract tax deductions to determine your taxable income, and
- You don't simply multiply your tax bracket by your taxable income. The government divides your taxable income into chunks and taxes each chunk at the corresponding rate.

Example:

For a single tax filer with a taxable income of $50,000, the bracket they would fall under would be 22%. This individual would be charged at different rates in different brackets:

You would pay 10% on the first $10,275 and 12% on the chunk of income between $10,276 and $41,775. Then you would pay 22% on the rest since some of the $50,000 taxable income is included in the 22% tax bracket.

Using the information above, you can now determine the tax bracket that you fall within. Then, assess what portions of your taxable income will be broken into. This will give you an idea of how the government will calculate your taxes.

Difference Between Tax Deductions and Tax Credits

Tax deductions and tax credits reduce your tax bill in different ways, so incorporating both into your planning can create an effective tax strategy.

What is the difference between tax deductions and tax credits?

Tax deductions are expenses that you have incurred during the tax period that you can subtract from your income. Deductions effectively reduce the amount of taxable income. Personal exemptions are one of the deductions that can be found on federal income tax returns. The following can be claimed as deductions:

- Donations to charity institutions recognized by the government
- Medical expenses
- Contributions to funds recognized by the government
- Mortgage loan interest
- Costs for dental procedures
- Schooling and fees
- Donations to a traditional IRA
- Donations to a health savings account
- Moving costs for new job possibilities
- Job search costs
- Teacher's educational costs
- Residential and real estate taxes

Tax Credits are a dollar-for-dollar reduction in the amount of taxes you owe. A common example is a child tax credit. Simply this means that should you receive a credit of $500, then you will be saving $500 on your tax return. Some of the common credits that you can apply for are:

- Earned Income Tax Credit (EITC): Designed for low to moderate-income individuals
- Lifetime Learning Credit
- Saver's Tax Credit: Based on contributions to retirement savings
- Residential Energy-Efficient Property Credit: Designed for individuals who are focused on making their homes more environmentally friendly

Tax Deductions vs. Taxable Income

Let's use an example of an annual gross income (AGI) of $100,000

Tax deduction: $10,000

- You would subtract $10,000, leaving you with $90,000 to be taxed. Say the tax rate is 25% (remember that the US uses a progressive tax system, this is just an example). That comes to a tax bill of $22,500.

Tax credit: $10,000

- You don't subtract any money from your AGI, leaving you with $100,000 to be taxed at 25%. That's a calculated tax of $25,000. You then subtract your tax credit, leaving you with a tax bill of $15,000.

The tax credit, in this case, saves you thousands of dollars more than the deduction would.

Standard Deductions and Itemizing

Standard deductions: This is a flat-dollar tax deduction set out each year by Congress. The deduction you qualify for depends on your filing status.

In 2021 the deductions were as follows:

- Single: $12,550
- Married, filing jointly: $25,100
- Married, filing separately: $12,550

- Head of household: $18,800

Standard deductions increase should you become blind or reach the age of 65 or older. It also increases by $1,650 if you are single or the head of the household and $1,300 if you are married or a widow(er).

A standard deduction:

- Allows you to take a tax deduction even if you have no expenses eligible for claiming itemized deductions.
- Cancels the need to itemize deductions.
- Allows you to avoid keeping records or receipts of your expenses in case you get audited.

Taxpayers who are not eligible for standard deductions are:

- A married individual who files separately, whose spouse itemized their deductions.
- Individuals who file for a term less than 12 months.
- A nonresident individual or a dual-status individual during the year.

Itemization: Rather than taking the standard deduction, you take individual tax deductions that you qualify for. People tend to itemize if their itemized deductions will add up to more than the standard deduction. This option takes longer to do your taxes, and you have to prove you qualified for those deductions. Itemized deductions reduce your adjusted gross income (AGI). Unlike standard deductions, the dollar amount differs between taxpayers.

Tip: A key part of determining this is to track deductions throughout the year. This will prevent you from having to go back through a year's worth of records when tax season rolls around.

Tip: You can itemize on your state tax return even when you take the standard deduction on your federal tax return.

Itemized deductions may make sense if you:

- Have itemized deductions that are worth more than your standard deductions.
- Have large cash expenses related to medical or dental procedures.
- You Paid mortgage interest and taxes on your home.
- Had large uninsured casualty or theft losses.
- Made large contributions to charity.
- Have gambling losses.
- Have other allowable deductions worth just over the amount of $3,000.

Hold Onto Your Tax Records

Keeping tax returns and any associated documents is critical if you're ever audited. The IRS has three years to decide whether to audit your return, so you should keep your records for at least that long, if not longer.

If you have ever wondered how long records should be kept for tax purposes, then here is a brief breakdown of what the IRS requires:

Three Years

- The IRS has three years to decide to audit your return in a typical tax filing situation. This means that records must be kept for a minimum time of three years from the date that you filed your return. Holding onto your tax records for three years gives you time to claim any refund or credit due to you from the IRS.
- If you file a claim for a credit or a refund after your original return, you should also hold onto those records for a minimum time of three years. From the date that you paid the tax that was due, the limit could be shifted to two years if this date is later than the three-year limit.

Six Years

- If you do not include all your earnings, the window for the IRS to do a potential audit stretches to six years, so this means you would need to hold on to your records for that time frame.
- Should you report your income leaving out more than 25%, the limitations are doubled. The IRS can then decide to audit any time within a six-year time frame to audit your return. You would need to have

access to your tax return documents for six years should they come knocking.

Seven Years

- You can write off losses from worthless security if a stock bet doesn't pay off, yet if you do, you would need to hold onto those records for a minimum time of seven years. That is the window in which the IRS may decide to evaluate your bad investment.
- When writing off bad debt, the same time frame applies.

Indefinitely

There are, in some cases, instances where you would need to hold onto documents for an undetermined amount of time or even forever:

- If someone commits tax fraud, there are no limitations on audits. Should the IRS suspect illegal information on a tax return, they can start investigating the activity at any time, not just within the time frames mentioned above.
- Should you miss a tax return or have not filed one, you would need to hold on to those documents indefinitely. For example: Should you have taken a year or two off without earning an income to take care of a loved one and you have nothing to file, you

would need to prove why. It will short-circuit a detailed IRS examination.

Records You Need to Hold Onto

Income

- W-2 Forms
- Bank statements
- 1099-MISC
- 1099-INT
- 1099-DIV
- Brokerage account
- Alimony obtained
- K-1 forms

Expenses and Deductions

- Receipts
- Invoices
- Alimony paid
- Charity statements
- Gambling losses

Home

- Closing statements
- Purchase and sale invoices
- Records of insurance
- Property tax assessments

Retirement Accounts

- Form 5498 (IRA contributions)
- Form 8606 (Nondeductible IRA contributions)
- 401(k) statements
- Distribution documentation
- Annual accounts

Additional Investments

- Transaction information (Including individual purchases or sale receipts)
- Annual accounts

If you decide to get rid of the supporting documents, you should still keep a copy of every year's tax returns. This includes your 1040 form and any associated schedules that you've sent to the IRS for that year. They are often needed if you are considering applying for a loan or any other financial assistance.

How Should Records Be Kept?

It's not just about keeping all that paperwork but how you should store them:

- There is no predetermined way that these records should be kept or stored. You can store them in any way that you find more convenient to you, as long as you have access to them should the IRS ask to view them. Many taxpayers prefer to keep digital records of all their tax returns as they are easier to access.

- Keeping all your financial records electronically could save you a lot of space and can save you the stress of wondering how long those records should be saved. You should just ensure that when you choose to save your documentation in an electronic format, it still meets the same standards as hard copies that the IRS requires. Simply said, that means that the records are kept for a certain time frame and that the electronic format is also available for that amount of time.

The Cashflow Quadrant

With this concept, each quadrant represents a different way to generate income. Depending on your financial situation, you can fall into one quadrant or multiple quadrants. The cash flow quadrant is split into four types of people, with two in each category.

The Left Side

The left side of the quadrant represents the Es and the Ss. These are individuals who are prone to paying the most taxes and who give up their time for money. Each one of these individuals has a different mindset.

E-Employee

Employees are individuals who have a job where they earn an income. Although the job is owned by a business, this could be a single person or a large corporation. An employee gives their time, energy, and skills in exchange for a paycheck and perhaps benefits. Employees often have a lack of control over their income, and this is the primary problem. However, security is one of the most important things to an employee. Many employees don't understand why people would want to be business owners or investors; it is a very big risk to them. Employees tend to stray away from putting themselves at risk; they generally aren't interested in learning about money or how it works. They would rather learn the skills needed to get a steady, higher-paying work opportunity with better benefits. Employees would rather look for a higher-paying job than make money for themselves. The amount of money you make is variable, but when you stop working, your income flow stops too.

S-Self-Employed

The S quadrant are employees who have grown tired of having absolutely no control over their finances. These are individuals who own their job. The self-employed quadrant is individuals who don't make good employees because they believe that there is no one who can do the work better than they can. Even though they still look for security, they are not afraid of taking risks or working for themselves. These individuals like the feeling of being in control of their future. Some S quadrant categories are doctors, lawyers, dentists, accountants, and various other service-based businesses and consultants. They have a very hard time delegating to others due to their extremely high standards of work. Hiring employees is also a challenge because they feel that no one can compare to them. This means they own a job, not a business, but just like employees, once they stop working, their income stops as well. When self-employed people need more money, they look for ways to earn more hours that they can bill for. Self-employed individuals often earn a larger income but with this comes more responsibility. This means working harder and longer over a more extended period, leading to burnout and fatigue.

The Right Side

The right side of the quadrant consists of the Bs and Is. They are individuals who pay fewer taxes and are more likely to create or invest in assets that increase income even when they are asleep.

B-Business Owner

Business owners don't own a job; they own a system and lead people or a product that produces income. Business owners are prone to hiring employees because they know that being successful without them is very difficult. They look for individuals who have the skills to complete business tasks and have more talent and skills than themselves. Delegation is a big part of a business owner's mindset, and they do not want to keep all the work for themselves. Successful business owners have the confidence to leave their business for an extended period while knowing that the business will still be running and profitable when they return.

They are considered risk-takers, but they believe that being an employee is riskier because employees have no control. A business owner has all the power as they have the final decision regarding the hiring and firing of employees. Should the economy fall, a business owner can make more money by either creating a new product or taking on a new system that will bring in more money.

I-Investor

Investors typically own assets that produce earnings. This quadrant offers passive income to the individuals involved in it. Individuals in this quadrant are those who were involved in one of the previous three quadrants, have earned an income, and now let their money work for them. These individuals are considered to have the highest financial education. They find assets that provide constant income streams that form part of cash flow, and they usually use the money of other individuals to obtain more assets. They also use the income obtained to gain access to more assets and, by doing this, grow their wealth through the velocity of money. They gain benefits with tax breaks, don't have to work if they don't want to, and they don't have to deal with employees. Investors look for opportunities to obtain assets that increase passive income. Investors and business owners in the B quadrant often walk alongside each other because investors buy shares from the owners in the B quadrant.

Financial independence has multiple paths, although most of them lead to the right side of the quadrant. It all depends on you. You would need to start learning the skills and mindset required and start moving to the right side.

Choosing Security Instead of Freedom

Poor or middle-class individuals either hold steady with their income, or their income has decreased over the past couple of years. Those on the left side believe that business owners and investors are living in security. These individuals living on the left side of the quadrant generally pay more taxes and higher interest on the debt. Understanding financial intelligence will help you understand why the Es and Ss are some of the poorest people and why they don't get rich.

How Do You Become Rich?

The amount of money you make is not what makes you rich; it's the amount of money you invest and save that makes you rich. Individuals on the right side of the quadrant pay fewer taxes, know how to make money from debt, and dodge inflation. Above all else, the right side quadrant keeps and makes more money than employees and self-employed individuals. The left side quadrant individuals work for an earned income, and this is classified as the highest taxed income. There are almost no tax shelters for this type of income. Earning a passive income gives you the least taxed income. There are also many more tax breaks that count to their advantage.

Shifting From Left to Right

The first step to moving from the left quadrant to the right quadrant is changing your mindset. Three things are seen as determining factors:

- Maintaining a long-term vision and plan
- Believing in delayed gratification
- Using the power of compounding in their favor

Individuals who were classified as wealthy and let themselves become poor had these three factors playing a role:

- Short-term vision
- The desire for instant gratification

- Abused the power of compounding

Moving quadrants starts with acquiring assets that can provide a passive income instead of creating a pattern of living paycheck to paycheck. You need to start small and have patience when moving, and then you can sit back and watch as your wealth grows.

In the following chapters, you will learn how to reduce your taxes by taking advantage of the provisions laid out in the tax law.

2

BALANCING YOUR ASSETS

T his chapter covers the different asset classes you should be aware of when investing.

Asset Classes

Before you can begin making the most of your tax deductions, you need to understand the asset class that you fall within. Different asset classes have different tax implications because the gains produced by these asset classes are taxed differently.

An asset class is defined as a "grouping of investments that exhibit similar characteristics and are subject to the same laws and regulations."

Understanding Asset Classes

The asset class is the grouping of comparable financial securities. These include IBM (International Business Machines), MSFT (Macalester Students for Fair Trade), and AAPL (American Association of Professional Landman) are all groups of stocks. Asset classes, as well as their categories, are often put together. There are often little correlation and a negative correlation between different asset classes. This is integral in investing. The three main asset classes are equities (stocks), fixed income (bonds), and cash equivalents/money market instruments. More recently, real estate, commodities, futures, and other financial derivatives, as well as cryptocurrencies, have also been added to the asset classes. Investment assets include tangible and intangible instruments that investors purchase or sell with the hopes of gaining additional income on a short or long-term basis. Various asset classes should reflect different risk and return investment characteristics as well as perform differently in various market environments. Diversifying asset classes could reduce portfolio risk and, in return, maximize returns.

For diversification purposes, financial advisors use investment vehicles as asset class categories. Each asset class has a different income stream and degree of risk, and for that reason, an investor could benefit immensely by combining assets from different asset classes.

Investing Strategy

It would be beneficial to apply investment strategies that focus on alpha investments to achieve alpha returns.

Different investment strategies focus on various factors like growth, value, income, or other factors that identify and categorize investment options. Valuation metrics like earnings-per-share growth (EPS) or price-to-earnings (P/E) are often criteria linked to performance. Some analysts are more concerned with the asset type or class than they are with the performance of the asset. Investing in the same asset class will produce the same cash flows.

The following asset classes are the most liquid asset classes as well as the most quoted asset classes:

Asset Class Types

- Equities (stocks)
- Contracts (fixed-income securities)
- Cash or marketable securities
- Commodities

The alternative asset classes include:

- Real estate
- Valuable inventory like artwork, stamps, and various tradeable collectibles.
- Hedge funds
- Venture Capital
- Crowdsourcing
- Cryptocurrencies

An asset's illiquidity does not show its return potential, but it may mean that it will take more time to sell the asset and earn an income. The assets mentioned above are also classified as the most popular classes. Asset classes are used by financial advisors when helping investors to diversify their portfolios and maximize their returns. You must invest in the right asset classes to maximize your tax savings. This will make or break your chances of success.

Four Main Asset Classes

The four main asset classes we're concerned with are business, real estate, paper assets, and commodities, although there are many more. It's important to look at different asset classes because having a diverse portfolio is essential. Within each asset class, there are hundreds of niches, which are your specific investments within the class.

Paper Assets

- These include stocks, bonds, mutual funds, retirement accounts you can invest with, stock futures, and foreign exchange.
- It also includes real estate investment trusts (REITs) and exchange-traded funds (EFTs).
- Most people invest in paper assets (i.e., the stock market) because they are easy to get in and out of. They are mostly liquid and require a low financial IQ.
- Now, you may already have a portfolio put together that is diversified among your paper assets-but if you aren't dividing your investments across those four classes, you are missing out on huge savings.

- This asset class includes the following most popular niches:
- Stock trading
- Stock options
- Bonds
- Annuities
- Whole life
- Universal life
- Foreign exchange
- Mutual funds
- Private equity
- EFTs

Commodities

- Generally a capital gains investment where you sell investments at a higher price than what you paid for them: Long-term capital gains are gains on investments you owned for more than one year and are subject to a 0%, 15%, or 20% tax rate depending on your level of taxable income. However, capital gains or loss investments generally don't generate passive income.
- Cryptocurrency is an emerging part of this asset class as well.
- These include Bitcoin, Ethereum, and Litecoin.
- Cryptocurrency is based on real people's money because it is created by humans and is completely separate from any government entity.
- They have a lot in common with traditional forms of money, even though they trade the same as paper

assets. They also store wealth, provide a unit of account, are divisible and transferable.

- Investors can buy the actual physical asset, purchase futures contraction at an exchange/brokerage, or buy the digital asset linked to the price of a commodity.
- Commodities include the following most popular niches:
- Oil and gas
- Mining
- Timber
- Farming
- Ranching
- Orchards
- Precious metals
- Utilities
- Renewable energy
- Horticulture

Business

- There are two ways to utilize this asset class: You either invest in your own business or invest in someone else's private business/company. The hope is that a return will be generated for you, the business, and any investor.
- You will need to research: The business itself, the partners, the financing, and the business and management team.
- Business assets include the following popular niches:

- MLM
- Online
- Retail
- Wholesale
- Manufacturing
- Professional services
- Restaurant
- Construction
- Personal services
- Sales

Real Estate

- Real estate may be your asset class, while your niche is single-family homes, or apartment buildings, or condos, and so forth.
- These investments either produce cash flow from rental properties (your net profit each month) or capital gains (a one-time profit from buying and selling a property).
- Real estate includes the following popular niches:
- Single-family
- Plexes
- Multi-family
- Back office
- Retail
- Industrial
- Office
- Strip mall
- Homebuilding
- Senior living

Asset Class Characteristics

Equities (Stocks)

- Part shares of ownership in a publicly-traded company
- High return, high risk
- The return consists of capital gains and income
- Sensitive to the economic cycle
- High liquidity and low transaction costs
- Subclasses: Value cv growth, small vs. large-cap, by region, by sector

Fixed Income

- Debt
- Lower return, lower risk than equities
- The return consists of capital gains and income
- Sensitive to interest rates
- Sensitive to issuer's ability to repay = credit risk
- Subclasses: By maturity, fixed vs. floating interest rate, government vs. corporate bonds, the latter further by sector, credit risk/rating

Cash and Cash Equivalents

- No risk, no return
- Perfect liquidity

Commodities

- Subclasses: energy, agriculture, industrial metals, precious metals
- High risk, lower return than equities
- Perfect for diversification and inflation hedge
- Correlation to equities and sensitive to economic cycle variations
- Agriculture commodities are subject to specific factors
- High seasonal returns
- Storage costs and pleasurable yield
- Liquidity variations

Real estate

- Lower risk and sometimes lower return than equities
- Leverage in the form of mortgages
- The return consists of capital gains and income
- Good inflation hedge
- Low liquidity, high trade costs, related charges, and taxes
- Subclasses: Land, residential, commercial
- Sensitivity to the economic cycle and correlation to equities varies
- Location is important
- Maintenance cost
- Unique risks

Infrastructure

- Example: Roads, railroads, airfields, water/energy production, storehouse, and disbursement
- Smaller return and smaller risk than equities
- Excellent inflation hedge
- Low relationship to equities, low sensitivity to the economic cycle
- Characteristics are similar with real estate.
- Typically long-term horizon.

Private Equity

- Like equities, it represents a proprietorship stake in an organization
- Unlike equities, it's not tradeable on public exchanges
- Comparable and often higher than public equities, but so is the risk associated
- Lower liquidity
- Unlike public equities, it lacks instant input in real-time stock prices, which can lead to underrating volatility/risk.
- Due diligence is hard but more important than with publicly traded equities.
- Passive or active
- Subclasses: Venture capital, leveraged buyouts, distressed, some types close to real estate, and corporate debt

Hedge Funds

- A diverse group that overspreads with many other asset classes
- Subclasses: Equity directional, corporate restructuring, relative value, macro, quant
- Risk, return, compatibility to equities, and acuteness to market cycle varies, depending on style
- Lower liquidity often has lock-up periods, notice periods, restoration penalties
- Higher administration and execution fees

Art and Collectibles

- Diverse and unique
- Represents value not related to purely financial gain to the holder
- Very low liquidity, lucid, and counterproductive markets
- Low correlation to equities and low sensitivity to the economic cycle
- Inflation hedge
- Typically long-time horizon

Insurance

- The main role is risk management and diversification
- Payoff subject to certain terms
- Low relationship to other asset classes
- Abnormal return allocation: Highly positive skewness and kurtosis.

Asset Classes and Diversification

Understanding exactly under which asset class an investment falls is not quite as necessary, but you need to understand that there are broad, general categories of investments. This is important, especially for diversification purposes. You would need to divide your investments across different asset classes to minimize your risk. There will be instances where equities may not be performing, but on the other side, real estate, bonds, and commodities may be performing great. Spreading your investments through different asset classes is often referred to as asset allocation.

Asset Allocation and Risk Tolerance

Choosing the right trade means you would need to have a basic understanding of the various asset classes available. Your risk tolerance and investment goals will play a significant role in your decision when you employ asset allocation. Should you be wary of high risks, then you may want to invest in safe asset classes. Holding a selection of large-cap, mid-cap, and small-cap stocks is how most investors prefer to diversify their investments. Those individuals who have the money to spend may be more open to diversification and be focused on trying to identify asset classes that offer the highest returns.

Financial Freedom Through Asset Classes

The financial gain you get from the different asset classes is based on your personal choice and your financial goals. You do not want to invest in something that does not interest you, and you aren't interested in learning about it. The best advice for investing is to choose something that you are passionate about; for example, if you love the idea of buying, renovating, and then selling houses (also called flipping houses), that could be something to consider. This is the key to staying motivated with your investments, but keep in mind that diversifying your portfolio could still increase your income. To financial planners and advisors, diversification is directly related to various stock sectors like a large-cap, small-cap, blended, blue-chip, high tech, or alternative energy.

After considering investing in your financial future, keep in mind to start small and use the Triple-A Triangle: Aspire, Acquire and Apply. Set goals for yourself, research everything, and then increase your financial education before taking action. Many women have changed their financial situation through investment, and I think anyone can if you set your mind to it.

Why Is a Balanced Portfolio Important?

A balanced portfolio helps you invest for maximum gain at a risk level that you're comfortable with. As mentioned before, having diverse investments is an excellent way to make sure your money is being put to good use and all your eggs aren't being kept in one basket. However, the small investor recognizes that she doesn't want to divide her attention among too many different things. When you focus your attention on one or two asset classes, you'll educate yourself more about the ins and outs of that particular asset type. The more educated you are, the greater your rate of return.

This results in your risk decreasing as your control increases, which will allow you to further reduce your taxes. By having control over your portfolio, you'll be able to make the necessary adjustments as they arise. You're already invested in one asset class, your business. That's the asset that will take up most of your time, understandably, and you'll want to invest in another asset class that will take your excess profits. This keeps your profit invested, not taxed; Real estate and paper assets are some of the best ways to do this. By focusing your efforts, you can reduce your timeline to financial freedom from 30-40 years to just 7-10 years when you make wise investment choices and manage your money in the right way.

Think of a balanced investment portfolio as a net under a tightrope to your financial future. It keeps you safe should you fall. Technically you will be able to earn more when investing in the best asset class, but you would need to make sure you know what you are doing. You need to feel comfortable with the upside risk and be able to handle the downside risk. Be careful not to invest too aggressively and then sell your assets when they drop beyond your comfort level, as you might just lose out on great potential gains that asset can provide you with. Balanced portfolios help investors find investments that can give them maximum profit while managing the risk of potential risk. This also helps prevent panic selling which results in long-term gains.

As certain assets start gaining more value, it's time for you to rebalance your portfolio. You will lose out on long-term gains if you do not rebalance your portfolio in time; you would want to make your money last. Selling assets that are getting too big for your portfolio could help you balance out your portfolio; as soon as you do that, you can reinvest in underrepresented asset classes. As investment starts gaining momentum for potential gain, it also gains a higher potential risk.

To rebalance your portfolio, you would need to consider selling those assets that are currently at a higher gain potential and buying assets that are still in the process of growing. This strategy is called "selling high, buying low."

When looking at your portfolio, answer these questions to yourself:

- Are the assets that are currently in your portfolio performing to your satisfaction?
- Is your portfolio balanced enough, or do you have to consider rebalancing it?

How can your portfolio become unbalanced?

Should your ideal portfolio consist of 60 percent small businesses and 40 percent paper assets, and one of your small business investments may triple in value overnight. This could cause your scales to tip. This could mean that your investments could now consist of 75% of your portfolio, and your paper assets have decreased to 25%. The same risks still exist. Should you decide to leave your investments untouched, you could be susceptible to higher risk, which would mean that you would need to reevaluate and rebalance your portfolio.

Achieving a Balanced Portfolio

A balanced portfolio assists you in reducing the risk of making long-term investment decisions. It helps you continue making wise decisions, which grows your wealth. Answer the following questions when you need to rebalance your portfolio:

- Are the assets that are currently in your portfolio performing as they should?
- What do I need to do to rebalance my portfolio?
- Is it necessary for my portfolio to be rebalanced?

Choosing Your Niche

Before choosing your perfect niche for investing, you would need to consider your goals and personal interests. This isn't to say that you must be fascinated by commodities to invest in them, but if you can find an asset niche that interests you, you'll enjoy keeping up with it more. For example, some investors may like the experience of owning an apartment complex, while others would rather invest in a real estate investment trust (REIT).

Picking a profitable niche or industry could be a bit challenging at times, but you would need to start by looking into different industries and perhaps your favorite companies. Investing and specializing in stocks that you are familiar with will pay off in the long term. Start by looking at products you use daily, industries you naturally follow due to a hobby that you enjoy researching, or the industry you are currently working in.

When considering your niche, try following these tips:

- Look for a niche that provides a daily or monthly income.
- Choose something that is currently in demand in the markets.
- Choose a niche that gives you complete control over your income.
- The niche needs to allow you to own investments rather than working through another individual partnership or LLC.
- Choose a passive income niche; passive income is usually considered to be taxed at lower rates.

Let's take the real estate investing niche as an example:

Real Estate Investing

Real estate investing is an excellent alternative to stocks and bonds and a great way of getting started to increase your success. It can be a bit overwhelming at first, but as soon as you do your research, you may find it easier than you expected. The first mistake you can make when choosing a real estate niche is jumping from one to the other, which could cause you not to close a deal. As soon as you put your mind on one niche, you can focus all your energy on it and learn as much as you can and be the best possible at it. Real estate is a physical asset that you can touch and see. You will be able to calculate whether you are making a good investment or not versus stocks where multiple variables need to be considered and you don't have much control over your returns. Here are a few niches to consider when looking into real estate investing:

Raw Land: This is defined as an open piece of land. This can be improved with utilities and be sold at a higher price or divided and sold separately. You can also sell with landowner financing, which provides you with a passive income. This could, in some cases, be better than owning a rental property, and you have no repairs to worry about.

Mobile Homes: Mobile homes require little to no out-of-pocket funds and can be a great source of income. Mobile homes are considered a vehicle; you can buy the mobile home with the land or just purchase the unit as a mobile home park. You will be able to sell it or rent it as an exit strategy.

Single-Family: Possibly the most common investment for investors. You can purchase, fix, sell, or rent it.

Duplex/Triple/Quads: These properties usually consist of two to four units. They are excellent investment sources because they can bring in multiple flows of income. Some individuals use one unit as their primary residence and then rent out the rest. The income received from the remaining units usually pays for the mortgage and creates extra income.

Small Apartments: These are properties that consist of five or more units. This is an excellent source of income, but the cost of running is generally higher than, for example, single-family homes because of the number of units. You could perhaps require a management company and someone that could do frequent repairs. In this case, the benefits outweigh the negatives. Individuals interested in investing in this type of property often understand this and are often willing to obtain some type of owner financing, so they don't have to pay the entire amount out of pocket. You can be creative with this niche, and sellers are often willing to work with you.

Some other niches available when looking into real estate and something you might want to learn more about include:

- Large apartments
- Commercial properties
- Tax liens
- Notes

3

MASTER DEDUCTIONS AND CREDITS

This chapter covers common itemized deductions and tax credits that you may qualify for. At this point, you want to determine whether you are eligible for any tax deductions, tax credits and if you should itemize them when you file your income tax return.

Common Itemized Deductions and Credits

At this point, you know what tax deductions are, and you have identified a niche that seems appealing and lucrative. Remember that deductions reduce taxable income, while credits reduce your tax bill. Some of the most common itemized deductions and credits are:

Property Taxes

Under the Tax Cuts and Jobs Act (TCJA), all state and local income taxes (SALT), including property taxes, are limited to $10,000 in deductions.

- The SALT deduction

State and Local tax deduct lets you deduct state local property tax payments, including your income or sales taxes. This is considered an itemized deduction; this means that your deductions should be over a certain amount when you claim it.

Mortgage Interest

Mortgage interest deduction allows you to deduct your interest; this includes your private mortgage insurance premiums. You would, however, need to itemize this deduction to claim it. Some individuals don't need to itemize after the 2017 tax reform.

State Taxes Paid

This is capped at $10,000 and includes all state and local income taxes.

Real Estate Expenses

These include mortgage insurance premiums, mortgage interest, and real estate taxes that you paid during the year.

Charitable Contributions

You can deduct charitable contributions of cash of up to 60% of your adjusted gross income. Donations of items or property are also considered itemized deductions. You would need to keep the receipts of purchases made for donation purposes because the IRS requires written confirmation for charitable deductions.

Medical Expenses

Medical expenses are categorized as itemized deductions; this means that you should only deduct them if your itemized deductions combined are more than your standard deductions ($12,550 for single filers, $25,100 for joint filers). You can only deduct the percentage of your medical and dental costs that is more than 7.5% of your adjusted gross income.

Lifetime Learning Education Credits

Who is eligible for LLC?

To be eligible, a student must:

- Be enrolled or taking courses at an eligible educational institution
- Taking higher education courses or courses to get a degree or other recognized education credential or to get or improve job skills
- Be enrolled at the beginning of the given tax year

The academic period can be semesters, trimesters, quarters, or any other period of study. This could also include summer school sessions. The academic periods are set out by the various schools and schools that make use of clock or credit hours and do not have academic terms may treat their payment periods as an academic period.

When filling for this credit, a student will receive a Form 1098-T, Tuition statement from the school they are studying at by no later than the 31st of January. This statement assists with figuring out your credit. Although an amount will be stated on the statement, that may not be the amount you could be eligible to claim.

The maximum amount of expenses you can deduct is up to $10,000 for an unlimited number of years, although the maximum you can receive as credit is $2,000 per tax return. Allows for a dollar-for-dollar reduction on the amount of taxes owed. If your modified adjusted gross income (MAGI) exceeds a certain threshold ($59,000 if single or $118,000 if married, filing jointly), the credit amount decreases. It is not available once your income exceeds $69,000 if single, $138,000 if married, filing jointly. This credit can't be claimed in the same year as the American Opportunity Tax Credit if the expenses are claimed as the Lifetime Learning Credit.

American Opportunity Tax Credit

Expenses can be included even if they are not paid directly to the school. Gives credits for the first four years of higher education, with a maximum credit amount of $2,500 for each eligible student. Note that if this credit brings your owed taxes to $0, 40% of any remaining amount of the credit (maximum of $1,000) can be refunded to you. Qualifying expenses include tuition, fee payments, and required books or supplies. This credit is reduced if the MAGI is between $80,000 but less than $90,000 for a single filer and $160,000 but less than $180,000 for married filing jointly.

Retirement Credits

The contributions you make to a retirement plan like a 401(k) or traditional/Roth IRA gives you a tax credit of 50%, 20%, or 10%, depending on your AGI. The maximum contribution amount that qualifies for the credit is $2,000 ($4,000 if married filing jointly), making the maximum credit $1,000 ($2,000 if married filing jointly).

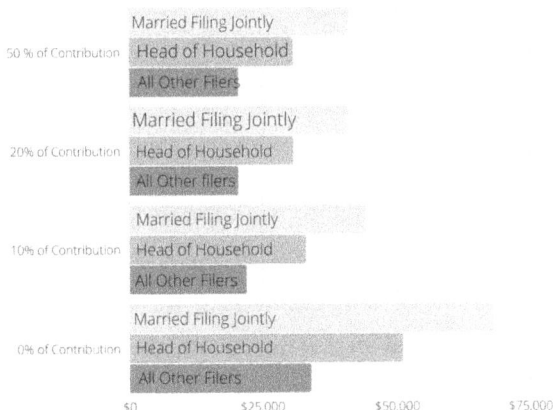

IRA Contributions

You can take IRA deductions should you contribute to a traditional IRA with income that you already paid income tax on. Income that you received from an employer who withholds income tax is included as part of this deduction. Traditional IRAs are tax-advantaged, meaning you don't pay income tax until you start withdrawing money from your retirement savings or investments. This may be reduced if your retirement plan is through your employer. The maximum contributions for 2021 in a traditional or Roth IRA are $6,000, plus another $1,000 for people who are 50+. These contributions are tax-deductible.

Self-Employed Health Care Premiums

Whether you itemize deductions or not, you can deduct 100% of the health insurance premiums that you pay monthly for yourself, your spouse, and your dependents. If you have kids and they will be under 27 at the end of 2021, you can also deduct their premiums even if they aren't dependents. This deduction can't be claimed if you are eligible to participate in a subsidized health plan from an employer of you, your spouse, dependents, or kids under 27.

Student Loan Interest

Interest from credit card debt used for educational payments can also be included; as long as these loans are used for yourself, a spouse, or a dependent, you may qualify for this credit. The maximum deduction is $2,500. If you are single with an AGI over $80,000 or married, filing jointly with an AGI of over $165,000, you can't take this deduction. Another deduction that you might want to consider is when your parents are paying the interest on your student loan because the IRS considers this deduction as a gift from your parents.

Business Travel Expenses

If you had to travel on assignment for work, you could deduct the necessary expenses from your taxes. Traveling away from home for your business, profession, or job is considered necessary and ordinary by the IRS as travel expenses.

Casualty, Disaster, or Theft Losses

You may be eligible to deduce casualty or theft losses related to your home and vehicle if the damage is due to a disaster declared by the president. There are special requirements for certain deductions as stated by the IRS. You need to verify IRS publications before claiming to ensure that you are eligible for the deduction.

Child and Dependent Care Credit

Parents actively looking for work and still spending money on their childcare can claim this credit. These costs may include a housekeeper, maid, cook, cleaner, or babysitter. However, this credit is only subject to 35% of your expenses to the maximum credit amount of $3,000 should you have one child under the age of 13 and $6,000 for two or more children. Form 2441 and Schedule Three is used to claim this credit, and the necessary information can be obtained from your care provider with Form W-10. This credit is not applicable should the care provider be a spouse or older dependent.

Child Tax Credit (CTC)

This credit is for taxpayers who pay for the majority of expenses for their children under the age of 17. You can qualify for a credit of up to $2,000, given you have an annual income of at least $2,500 to qualify. This credit can decrease when your gross income reaches a certain level: $400,000 for joint filers and $200,000 for all other filing statuses.

Additional Child Tax Credit (ACTC)

In addition to CTC, you can take the additional child tax credit that allows you to receive a refund if CTC brings your tax liability below $0. ACTC refund is only up to the value of $1,400 in this situation. You may be disqualified from the ACTC deductions should you receive an income from a foreign source.

Credit for Other Dependents (ODC)

This deduction is for dependents who cannot be claimed under the CTC or ACTC, and you can deduct up to $500 for every dependent. Contributions towards the care of a parent will qualify for this deduction. This deduction starts to fade away once your income reaches $400,000 for joint filers or $200,00 for other filing statuses.

Earned Income Tax Credit

This credit is primarily available for low-income and moderate-income taxpayers, while the highest amount of credit goes to taxpayers with dependents. This credit can be claimed using Form 1040, but you need to complete the Schedule EIC as well should you have a dependent. Established in 1975, the EITC is determined by income and phased in according to filing status. For 2021, a person must be at least 19 years old (unless a former foster youth or qualified homeless youth, which is age 18), and a student must be at least 24. There is no upper age limit.

If married, both spouses must have valid SSNs (Social Security Numbers) and have lived in the country for more than six months. If you are claimed as a dependent by another filer, you don't qualify. You do not qualify if you earned $10,000 or more in 2021 in investment income.

Overlooked Small Business Tax Deductions

- Startup and organizational costs

The costs that you have incurred before opening the doors of your business, like expenses used to explore business opportunities, can entitle you to a deduction in the first year of your business. The costs you incur before starting your business are deductible even though you would have to be operating a business to deduct these expenses. An amount of $5,000 can be deducted from your startup costs, but if the amount exceeds this amount, you will be able to amortize over a period of 15 years. There are, however, certain limitations should these costs be over the amount of $50,000.

- Inventory

Inventory items aren't immediately deductible; instead, businesses with inventory use accrual accounting methods and include their inventory items under the cost of goods sold category. This reduces the amount of income considered as sales. Many small businesses use cash accounting and prefer to treat inventory items as materials and supplies, which are deductible. Small businesses are defined as businesses with less than $25 million income over three years; there are also industry restrictions. Small businesses that can be eligible for these deductions are usually service-based businesses that have an inventory like beauty salons that do hair-cutting services and sell beauty products like shampoo and conditioner.

- Utilities

Business owners are able to deduct utilities as a business expense. These utilities could include telecommunication services, electricity, gas, trash, and water services. This could be a flat rate or based on usage. This usually appears on a utility bill with other general service charges.

- Insurance

Obtaining insurance for your business is unavoidable and something that every small business owner needs to consider at some point. These insurance premiums are tax-deductible and may include liability coverage, health insurance, workers' compensation, business interruption insurance, and other insurance types.

- Business property rent

Should you be self-employed and use your residence or other property for business purposes, you may be eligible to deduct a portion as a business expense. This can be done through the home office deduction.

- Auto expenses

One way of writing off car expenses is by taking a standard mileage deduction for a business trip. There is a yearly mileage reimbursement rate set out by the IRS. You need to report the number of miles you drove for business purposes when filing your return. Your reimbursement will be calculated as follows:

Business mileage x IRS standard mileage rate = Your mileage deduction.

For example, if the mileage reimbursement rate is 58 cents a mile, and you drive 10,000 miles in a tax year, your deduction will be $5,800.

10,000 x $0.58 = $5,800

Many business owners overlook the business mileage deduction because they don't understand what it is. You can build up business miles for driving your car for work purposes, except driving from your home to work premises. This means you are unable to deduct miles that have been used for commuting to work and back home.

- Rent and depreciation on equipment and machinery

Deductions on depreciation of equipment can be claimed on any equipment that your company owns and uses in the daily operation of your business. This deduction does not apply to equipment that is rented. The depreciated equipment should have a determined life span which should be more than one year. You should also be aware of the depreciation value of the equipment.

- Office supplies and furniture

Only furniture used for the operation of your business is deductible. These could include chairs, desks, office printers, other office electronics, shelving, and picture frames used in the office space only. This deduction assists small businesses by increasing their net income after tax; it also automatically decreases the amount of taxes you pay during the year in which you take the deduction.

- Software subscriptions

Subscriptions related to the business are deductible and are classified as a business expense. These subscriptions include

- Professional, technical, medical, or trade journals and magazines
- Professional material subscriptions
- Business plan phone
- Electricity, internet, and other phones for your home office
- Hosting fees for your website
- Professional subscriptions or organizations
- Advertising and marketing

Advertising is a crucial part of any new or small business. With the price of advertising growing significantly, it helps to know that this expense is fully deductible. Some of the expenses that can be deducted are website costs, digital advertising, etc.

- Travel expenses

You will also be able to deduct expenses for traveling with services like Lyft, Uber, taxis, and public transport. This deduction is the same as deducting the expenses for business mileage; this means the expenses would need to be for business purposes and not commuting to and from your place of business. Another traveling expense that is tax-deductible is paying for parking as well as highway tolls and feeding meters. This is applicable when you may be parking at an airport for a work trip or anywhere else for business purposes (except your place of work).

- Interest

Business interest expenses could be deductible as an ordinary business expense for certain businesses.

- Employee salaries (excluding sole proprietors, partners, and LLC members)

It's important to track expenses incurred when paying salaries to employees as well as paying for freelancers or independent contractors.

- Contracted labor

Contracted labor fees can be deducted as a business expense against your tax return; however, you would need to have a 1099 form for each contractor that you have paid $600 or more during the given year.

- Legal and professional fees

The moment legal and professional fees become necessary and are related to the daily running of your business, they become tax-deductible. These fees are related to attorneys, business coaches, financial planners, bookkeepers, and tax experts.

- Home office

Filing a home office deduction is a legal deduction and does not give off red flags, as many believe. The majority of businesses are home-based, and the IRS has created a new, simplified, home office deduction method. You need to make sure that you are truly entitled to this deduction before claiming it. The two conditions you need to adhere to are using space as your primary place of business or any other acceptable purpose and using the space regularly and exclusively for business purposes. Examples of 100% home office deductions are:

- Repairs to your home office (for example, painting, reflooring, installing light fixtures, patching walls, etc.)
- Maintenance on your home office (for example, hiring a cleaner)
- Office furniture and décor, ensuring these expenses are only used in your home office and not for personal use

Ensure that you use your business bank account when paying for these expenses so you can track your expenses and then treat them as such when doing your accounting.

- Medical reimbursement: If you offer a formal medical reimbursement plan to your employees, you can qualify for tax advantages

4

LOWER YOUR TAX BRACKET

This chapter explores the concept of income shifting/splitting, explaining what it is and how to do it.

Income Shifting

Income shifting is a relatively new concept. Yet it has been used by wealthy individuals for generations as a means of shielding their income from tax. Income shifting is a completely legal way of lowering your tax burden as long as you stay within the IRS guidelines.

Income shifting, also referred to as income splitting, transfers income from high to low tax bracket taxpayers. For example, shifting unearned investment income from a parent to a child.

Breaking Down Income Shifting

Today's most popular example is shifting unearned invest-ment income from a high tax bracket parent to a low tax bracket child. This is usually done via a trust or in the form of a gift. Kiddie tax needs to be taken into consideration when these shifts are made to curb the tax loophole.

High to Low Tax Bracket Income Shifting

Family-owned businesses may employ family members and hire relatives to enable the distribution of company earnings to low bracket relatives by paying them salaries. These salaries are then considered as business expenses if the amount and work performed are reasonable. Loans with no or below-market interests can also be helpful, as well as life insurance and annuity policies. These are, however, subject to the risk of imputed interest or gift reclassification. Income shifting can be used alone or in collaboration with income splitting to family limited partnerships (FLPs). This allows the owner to transfer business assets to FLPs and then sell, gift outright, or in trust, FLP interests to lower tax bracket relatives.

Income Shifting From Tax Inversion

A more conventional way is used to shift income from high to low tax jurisdictions. Tax inversion is the transferring of income-based assets to non-grantor trusts formed and residing in low tax states. Merging with a foreign company in a low tax rate country can produce the same results.

A Multinational Enterprise (MNEs) can further reduce taxes by shifting income domestically to their lower tax rate geographical business locations or offshore by making sales at transfer prices or factoring receivables to their low tax rate foreign affiliates.

Income Shifting Methods

Hiring Your Kids

Hiring your children to work in your business, given that they are legitimate employees, is a viable tax-saving strategy. You can deduct their salaries as business expenses from your business income. This can give you significant self-employment tax and ordinary income tax savings.

Keep in mind:

- Your kids would need to be verified employees and perform work-related services. Tasks you can assign your child as doing are answering phones, filing documents, cutting grass, and trimming bushes outside of the business premises.
- The appropriate forms will need to be completed, and the child would need to be paid a reasonable salary for their tasks. The IRS would need to see the compensation as being reasonable; paying too high of a rate could potentially raise red flags.
- Having your child complete timecards as proof of hours of work is very beneficial and can be used as proof.

Not Claiming Your Child on Your Tax Return

Should you have a spouse, partner, child, stepchild, adopted child, foster child, younger sibling, elderly parent, grandparent, in-law, or other person living in your household that you are financially responsible for, you could claim them as a dependent. Although this could lower your tax liability status, consider these reasons to rather avoid it:

- When you are using education credits as an income-shifting strategy, you may not be able to claim the Hope or Lifetime Learning Credits for your college-age children. You may want to take them off as dependents when your children earn a taxable income from work or investments. You will be losing the benefit of our children's dependent exemption anyway. You may also elect not to claim your children as dependents, and they can claim the education credits on their income tax returns even if you paid their college tuition.
- Once an individual is earning more than the allowable amount, then they will be eligible to file their taxes, and when this happens, the taxpayer may not be reimbursed for money that they have spent to take care of that individual.
- It is essential to speak to a professional who is knowledgeable about IRS dependency laws when you are currently facing child custody issues. Your spouse may also claim a child as a dependent, which could result in the holding of your tax processing.
- You could reap tax benefits if you hire your parents, given they are in a lower tax bracket. When your parents are retired, this could mean they qualify for a low-income tax bracket. This means that you can

give a portion of your s-corporation, LLC, or Limited partnership to your parents, and the income from their share would go through their tax return at a lower tax rate. You will stay the majority and will still have complete control of the business.

- Depending on the type of business you own, you may need medical equipment or own your office building. You can use a sale-leaseback or gift leaseback as a tax-advantaged strategy if you own these items to get more capital or to shift income to a family member's tax bracket while adding more tax deductions to your return. Leaseback is when an owner and buyer/giftee enter into an agreement that the owner can lease the items back from the buyer/giftee. Equipment and real estate are the most common types of property used for this strategy.

- Year-end bonuses are considered supplemental income, and because of this, they can lead to a higher withholding rate. This means that you will receive less due to the higher tax that is charged on it. Higher-income taxpayers may lose certain tax deductions should their income reach a certain threshold. Moving your year-end bonus to the following year could be beneficial, especially if you receive productivity bonuses or call money during the year. You need to consider taking an increase in the current year instead of the following year.

- You can start deducting business expenses from the moment you open your business doors. If you can prove that the expenses are ordinary and necessary, then they become fully deductible against your business income. Meals, travel, vehicle costs, and medical expenses that you still have may also be deductible before the company opens, given the correct business structure is in place.

Some of the most popular income shifting methods:

- Employing family members
- Family partnerships
- Interest-free and below-market loans
- Gifting
- Sale- or gift-leaseback
- Trusts
- Life Insurance/annuities

Kiddie Tax

When using any of the above methods to shift income to a child, you must keep the kiddie tax in mind.

What Is Kiddie Tax?

The kiddie tax applies when a child has unearned income (like investment income). Children under the tax are generally taxed at their parent's tax rate on any unearned income over a certain amount.

- Currently, this amount is $1,900 (the first $950 is the tax fee, the next $950 is taxed at the child's rate)
- It applies to Those under the age of 18, Those whose earned income doesn't exceed half of their support, those ages 19 to 23 who are full-time students, and

whose earned income doesn't exceed half of their support.

How Does Kiddie Tax Work?

Kiddie tax has been designed to prevent parents from exploiting a tax loophole. When a child receives a large number of gifts or stocks, the child can realize any gains from the investments and then be taxed at a lower rate compared to their guardians. Unearned income below $1,100 is considered standard deductions, where the next $1,100 would be taxed at the child's tax rate, which is either very low or zero. Everything over the amount of $2,200 can be taxed at the guardian's tax rate, which could be as high as 37%.

Who and What Is It Applied to?

Kiddie tax is applied to children under the age of 18 of the tax year, also children who are full-time students and dependents between the ages of 19 and 24. However, this falls away should a child be under this age, married, and filing joint tax returns. Unearned income a child receives that is included under kiddie tax is interest, dividends, capital gains, rent, and royalties. A salary is not subject to the kiddie tax.

History of Kiddie Tax

Kiddie tax originally only provided coverage for children under the age of 14 because they could not work. This means that they only received income from dividends or interest. Tax authorities, however, realized that guardians took advantage of the situation and gave stock gifts to their older children. Any income exceeding the predetermined threshold is taxed at the parent's tax rate.

What Is Unearned income?

Unearned income is any source of income that is not obtained through wages or salaries. The following unearned income sources are considered when determining kiddie tax:

- Alimony payments
- Capital gains and capital gain distributions
- Ordinary dividends
- Pension and annuity income
- Rental income
- Royalties
- Taxable interest
- Taxable scholarships and fellowship grants not reported on Form W-2
- Taxable Social Security benefits
- Unearned income of any type that was received as a trust beneficiary
- Unemployment benefits

How to Report Kiddie Tax

There are two ways to report kiddie tax:

- The child can file their own tax return. Children who are still minors cannot complete the form themselves, so a parent or guardian needs to complete it on their behalf.
- A parent can include the child's income on their tax

return, although this is only available should the child's income be below $11,000.

Pros and Cons for Kiddie Tax Filing

Adding a child's income to a parent's tax return could simplify a family's tax situation. It could mean more forms and higher prices should a child's income be filed separately. Should a child earn an income and need to file, then adding the unearned income on their tax return becomes simpler than adding it to a parent's return. Children filing their tax returns could result in lower overall taxes. Should you be unsure how to submit your filing, you may want to consider testing out both and seeing which one results in less tax.

6 Steps to Shifting Income to Another Taxpayer

Step 1: Identify unused tax brackets

- Upper tax bracket, family business owners can shift income from business earnings distributions to low tax bracket relatives by hiring them to work for the business and paying them a salary.
- These unused tax brackets can be with your children, parents, relatives, etc.

Step 2: Hire your family

- Salaries are deductible as business expenses if reasonable for the amount and work performed. You can hire your children as employees of your family business, getting tax breaks for their salaries while also encouraging them to work and save money.

- The money that you pay them can then be used on vacations, extracurriculars, clothing, and other expenses that they incur.
- The tax code provides a Federal insurance Contributions Act (FICA) and Federal Unemployment Tax Act (FUTA) tax exclusion for unincorporated businesses that employ an owner's children.
- The earnings of a minor under 18 who is employed by a parent who owns a sole proprietorship or partnership are not subject to FICA (Social Security and Medicare Taxes).
- There is also an exclusion from FUTA (unemployment tax) for a business paying the owner's child who is under the age of 21.

Step 3: Explore trusts and gifts

- The Uniform Transfers to Minors Act (UTMA) and the Uniform Gifts to Minors Act (UGMA) are two ways to transfer unearned investment income from a high bracket parent to a low tax bracket child.
- What is the UGMA? It allows the property to be transferred to a minor without needing a formal trust, instead of having assets be managed by a custodian who the donor appoints. When minors come of legal age, they receive the property.
- What is UTMA? An extension of the UGMA, which

only covered cash and securities. This act allows a minor to receive gifts without the aid of a guardian or trustee. These can include money, patents, royalties, real estate, and fine art. Until the minor comes of legal age in the state, they can avoid tax consequences. The IRS allows for an exclusion from the gift tax of up to $15,000 per person for tax years between 2018 and 2021. Note: The minor's SSN is used for tax reporting purposes since they own the asset. This could have negative consequences when the minor applies for financial aid or scholarships.

- Differences between UTMA and UGMA. The UTMA includes a broader range of giftable assets and provides additional time for gifted assets to reach their maturity date, like with bonds. The UGMA requires that all assets are assumed by the minor once the minor becomes 18 years old.
- Pros and cons. The money contributed into the account is exempted from paying a gift tax of up to a maximum of $15,000 per year. Plus, any income on the contributed funds is taxed at the tax rate of the minor being gifted the funds. However, it can make the recipient less eligible for need-based scholarship programs.

Step 4: Consider family limited partnerships (FLPs)

- These are owned by family members and operate under the rules of limited partnerships. Parents will often form an FLP and transfer their assets to this entity.

- It can be used to shift current business income to lower-bracket family members. Children are treated like investors rather than owners. Each child can receive LP interests worth $15,000 from each parent as gifts, without federal gift tax consequences.
- Limited partners can also work in their business and be compensated for their services.

Step 5: Take advantage of interest-free and below-market loans

- Use a loan to a family member as an alternative to a gift
- Low interest means that the rate of interest is less than the applicable federal rate (AFR) set monthly by the IRS. Generally, the IRS will treat you as if you've received interest after the AFR if you loan money without charging at least the AFR.
- Generally, $10,000 or less loans will not result in imputed interest or reclassification as a taxable gift.

Step 6: Utilize annuities and life insurance

- You can purchase an annuity to reduce income taxes since the income generated by the annuity will accumulate tax-free until the funds are withdrawn.
- As long as you don't make any withdrawals, the interest is not taxable in the current year. Note: If the annuity payouts begin when you are older, you may be in a lower tax bracket by that point.

Make the Most of C and S Corporations

C and S corporations will be discussed in greater detail in chapter 7, but right now, we're going to look at some of the ways they can be utilized to lower your tax bracket.

C Corporations

- C corporations have more flexibility in determining their fiscal year, and income can be shifted more easily forward and backward.
- Shareholders of C corporations can act as salaried employees. These salaries and bonuses are subject to payroll taxes and Social Security and Medicare taxes; however, the corporation can fully deduct its share of payroll taxes. The company can also pay employees enough that no taxable profits remain at the end of the fiscal year, rather than paying out dividends that would be double taxed.
- C corporations are also taxed at a lower rate than other corporation types, which is particularly advantageous for business owners to reduce their overall tax liability.
- Fringe benefits offered by the C corporation to all employees can be written off under medical reimbursement plans and premiums for health, long-term care, and disability insurance. In contrast with S corporations, the shareholders deduct medical costs from gross income but have to declare the fringe benefits as income.

S Corporation

- Losses incurred by an S corporation will flow through to a shareholder's tax return.

S Corporations and C Corporations

- Another way to reduce your tax bracket is to have your S corporation and C corporation work with one another.
- Your S corporation can pay your C corporation for consulting and administrative services (payroll, HR, bookkeeping, etc.) This shifts the income from the S corporation to a lower corporate rate of only 21%.

Deferring Income Until After Year-End

By deferring your income to a later year, you might be able to maximize your tax liability and end up in a lower tax bracket.

Delay Collections: If you're self-employed, you can wait to collect money owed to you by sending year-end bills in late December so that you won't receive the payments until the following year.

Defer Compensation: It might be possible to have your employer wait until early the following year to pay you some of your year-end wages.

Maximize Retirement Savings to Reduce Your AGI: If you contribute the maximum amounts to certain retirement plans (401(k)s, IRAs, etc.), you can reduce your AGI for the year.

Prepaying Expenses: You can prepay some of your business expenses for future years, such as business insurance, rent on offices and equipment, and lease payments. However, the general rule is that you can't prepay expenses for a future year and deduct them from the current year's taxes. There are important exceptions called the 12-month rule:

- You can deduct a prepaid future expense in the current year if the expense is for a right or benefits that extend no longer than 12 months until the end of the tax year after the tax year in which you made the payment, whichever happens, earlier.
- The rule can be used for business insurance payments to terminate business contacts. It cannot be used to pay interest, loans, financial interest, furniture, equipment, or other long-term capital assets.

Note; If you choose to prepay expenses, be sure to have documentation that you sent the advance payment in case you are audited. Use US Postal Service mail with tracking or some other form of certified mail.

5

MORE ON TAX CREDITS

This chapter goes into greater detail about the tax credits available to small business owners and the eligibility requirements to qualify for them. While we covered some of the available tax credits in chapter 3, you'll want to be sure you're making the absolute most of the credits available to you as a small-business owner. The government wants people to work and contribute to the economy and offers several tax credits to encourage people to do this.

If you are eligible for more than one small-business tax credit, you must submit IRS form 3800 with your tax return. This form lists every small business tax credit that your company may qualify for. Although, there is a limit to the amount you can claim each year. Each tax credit requires its own form. To determine your business' limit:

- Add your net income and alternative minimum tax.

- Subtract the greater of either your tentative minimum tax for the tax year or 25% of the amount of your regular tax liability that's greater than $25,000.

Most Important Small-Business Tax Credits

Meant to encourage small business owners to provide paid leave to employees for the birth of a child, health emergency, or other reason covered by the Family and Medical Leave Act (FMLA).

Tax deductions and tax credits can both significantly reduce your tax obligations, although tax credits have an edge since they can earn you more refunds. Trying to stay up to date with available credits could become challenging at times, especially when other things need to be done, like running your business. Here are the most important types of tax credits.

General Business Tax Credit

This is a catchall tax credit consisting of several different individual tax credits. These credits are explained in more detail below; keep in mind that each one has its own form that needs to be completed.

Small Business Health Insurance Premiums

Health insurance can be expensive for small businesses as well as complicated to initiate. Although 55% of employees suggest that it is the most significant benefit that companies offer. This credit aims to alleviate this with a tax credit that will cover up to 50% of the premium amount for two years. To qualify for this credit, you will need to have:

- Fewer than 25 full-time employees
- Pay wages less than $51,600 per year
- Fund at least half of all your employee's health insurance
- Purchase your health insurance plan through Small Business Health Options Marketplace
- This credit is for companies that provide small-business health insurance to their employees

Paid Family and Medical Leave

This credit is available to companies that offer their employees paid family and medical leave. This credit covers 12.5% to 25% of what you paid to your employees for up to 12 weeks. This leave is considered in certain cases as unpaid, job-protected leave. This type of leave relates to the birth of a child, health emergency for family, or any other reason considered under the Family and Medical Leave Act (FMLA). Employers are eligible for this leave if they:

- Have a written policy that states employees are eligible for at least two weeks of paid family and medical leave per year.
- Pay employees 50% of their wages during this leave.

This credit is equivalent to 12.5% of the salaries that are paid to employees on family and medical leave during the given year. Should you pay your employees more than half of their wages during this period, then the credit will also increase. The credit is capped at 25% of the wages for businesses that pay employees 100% of their wages during their leave period. This credit is claimed using Form 8994.

Work Opportunity Credit

Companies that employ individuals who are struggling to get work opportunities elsewhere can gain credit from the Work Opportunity Tax Credit (WOTC).

There are ten categories that the IRS has defined of WOTC-eligible workers:

- Qualified IV-A Temporary Assistance for Needy Families (TANF) recipients
- Unemployed veterans, including disabled veterans
- Ex-Felons
- Designated community residents living in Empowerment zones or Rural Renewal countries
- Vocational rehabilitation referrals
- Summer youth employees living in Empowerment Zones
- Food stamp (SNAP) recipients
- Supplemental Security Income (SSI) recipients
- Long-term family assistant recipients
- Qualified long-term unemployment recipients

This credit depends on the category that the employee is considered under and how many hours they have worked during the tax year. You could potentially save up to $9,000 over a period of two years, depending on the wages that you are paying your WOTC pre-qualified employees. This credit is, however, capped off at $2,400 per worker. To optimize on this credit, Form 5884 would need to be completed.

Increasing Research Activities

Companies that have expenses related to research and development in the United States can qualify for this credit. Also referred to as the R&D Tax Credit. You need to have less than $5 million in gross receipts for the credit year to be eligible for this tax credit, also no more than five years of gross receipts. Some of the qualifying activities include:

- Streamlining internal processes
- Developing or improving technologies
- Applying for patents
- Developing new prototypes or models
- Developing proprietary products and seeking patents
- Developing a new manufacturing process or business process
- Improve product efficiency
- Improving quality control processes
- Environmental or certification testing

You can subtract up to 10% of your R&D costs from your tax should you qualify for this credit. Certain small businesses may use this credit to offset their alternative minimum tax as per the reforms enacted by the Protecting Americans from Tax Hikes Act (PATH). These businesses should be a non-publicly traded corporation, partnership, or sole proprietor. Businesses would need to supply project notes, process diagrams, lab results, etc. This credit is claimed by using Form 6765, which includes complete instructions on how to claim.

Disabled Access

This is meant to encourage companies to make their business locations accessible to customers with disabilities.

The Disabled Access Credit is available for any company that has spent money to make their business more accessible for disabled individuals. The following examples are considered by the IRS:

- Construct ramps for wheelchair access
- Provide text in braille
- Create accessible rooms, restrooms, and workspaces with wider doors
- Remove barriers and obstacles
- Install automatic doors

This credit would cover 50% of your expenses to a maximum amount of $5,000. Businesses should have less than $1 million in revenue or fewer than 30 full-time employees. You can cover up to 50% of the expenses incurred, ranging from $500 to $10,000. Form 8826 is used to claim this credit on your tax return.

Employer-Provided Childcare Facilities and Services

Aimed at businesses that pay for their employees' childcare expenses or help their employees obtain childcare. These expenses are only applicable to facilities whose primary function is the care of children. The following also needs to be taken into consideration when choosing a childcare facility:

Expenses incurred for the construction, remodeling, or expansion of a childcare facility. This is excluding an employee's primary residence.

- Expenses for the operation of an existing childcare facility, for example, caregiver wages.
- Expenses through a contracted qualified childcare facility
- Expenses incurred to provide childcare resources and referral through a contracted childcare provider

Employees realize a more significant benefit from the Employer-provided childcare tax credit than from the child and dependent care tax credit because they could claim this credit on their personal tax return as well. Employees can take a credit of up to $1,050 on their return should they pay $3,000 for childcare. This would mean that the employee only pays $1,950 for childcare services.

Qualifying businesses can claim up to 25% of their expenses on childcare, plus an additional 10% of the childcare resources and referral expenses. This is limited to $150,000 per year. All these facilities need to be qualified childcare facilities; this means they would need to comply with licensing requirements relevant to their location. Claiming this credit would require you to use Form 8882.

- The facility should have open-enrollment for all employees.
- Not discriminate against lower-earning employees.
- At least 30% of the enrolled children should be that of the employees currently working for the company.

Rehabilitation, Energy, and Reforestation Investment Credit

This credit is available to businesses who invest in the reforestation, building rehabilitation, and alternative energy used in their businesses. This credit is limited to 22% of their expenses for solar, fuel cells, and small wind technologies and up to 10% for geothermal, microturbines, and CHP and is limited to $10,000 per year. This credit can be claimed using Form 3468. The following energy-saving measures are considered when you are looking at claiming this credit:

- Solar energy is used to generate electricity, heat, or cooling of a business, provide hot water, or generate solar process heat
- The production or distribution of geothermal energy from rocks, water, or steam
- The property is depreciable and used in your business

The following eligible technologies make a company eligible for this credit:

- Solar technology
- Fuel cells

- Small wind turbines
- Geothermal systems
- Microturbines
- Combined heat and power (CHP)

Alternative Motor Vehicles, Electric Vehicles, and Alternative Fuel

A tax credit designed to encourage companies to use alternative fuel source vehicles. Your company could be eligible for a credit of up to $8,000, although this does not apply to hybrids or electric cars that use conventional fuel sources. The only vehicle currently recognized by the IRS is the Honda FCX Clarity, which uses hydrogen fuel cells. This tax credit needs to be kept in mind when a company purchases new vehicles.

If you produce/use alternative fuels in business, use an electric vehicle, or use a vehicle that runs on alternative energy, you may be able to claim some of this credit. Biodiesel and renewable diesel fuels credit. Alternative fuel vehicle refueling property credit. Biofuel producer credit. Qualified electric vehicle credit. Investment credit for rehabilitation and alternative energy.

Forms 8849, 4136, 6478, 8864, or 8896 are commonly used to claim the refund for alcohol, biodiesel, low-sulfur diesel, or renewable diesel. Alternative fuel vehicle refueling property credit is claimed using Form 8911, and qualified electric vehicle credit is claimed using Form 8834.

Employer Social Security and Medicare Taxes Paid on Certain Employee Tips

If your employees receive tips, you can claim a tax credit for the social security and Medicare payroll taxes you paid on those tips. This credit is reduced for businesses that don't pay their employees the federal minimum wage.

Small Employer Pension Plan Start-Up Costs and Auto-Enrollment

The government is aiming to help businesses to start a retirement program because they want individuals to begin planning for their retirement. This credit could save a company up to 50% of the ordinary and necessary eligible startup costs of starting a company-sponsored retirement plan. These costs include setup and administration fees and money used to educate employees about the program. This credit is only available to companies with 100 employees or less who will receive more than $5,000 in compensation from your company and is only available for the first three years. This credit is available to the following companies:

- Companies with fewer than 100 employees during the given year
- Companies that have not had a retirement plan in place for a period of at least three years for the same employees

Retirement plans that qualify under these credits are 401(k) plans, SEP IRA plans, and SIMPLE IRA plans. Self-employed individuals can benefit from the retirement savings contribution tax credit if they fall into a lower income bracket. Form 8881 is used to claim this credit.

New Markets

Supports businesses that invest in Community Development Enterprises (CDEs) and Community Development Financial Institutions (CDFIs) to help support low-income communities. The most eligible projects include:

- Fixing or building of educational facilities or community centers
- Fixing or building of hospital or healthcare facilities
- Fixing and flipping businesses that renovate residential properties
- Fixing or building of industrial buildings that create jobs
- Fixing or building of facilities for women, minorities, and other underserved communities

These projects need to be in 20% poverty rate areas, or where medium families with income less than 80% of the area median income are received. Form 8874 is used to file for this tax credit.

Qualified Business Income Deduction

Sole proprietors, S-corporations, and partnerships can deduct up to 20% of their qualified business income. There are, however, limitations on this amount, but any industry would be able to take this deduction given their income is under $157,500 if single and $315,000 if married.

Keep in mind when claiming tax credits that this is not a one-and-done activity. Every year, you need to review this to ensure you are still eligible for certain tax credits because they are subject to change. You could only be able to claim for certain things once, whereas once your business develops, you may be able to claim for things that were unavailable previously. Small business tax credits may be hard to parse and quite challenging to keep track of but are worth the effort. You would need to ensure your account process is as up-to-date as possible.

6

REAPING THE REWARDS OF REAL ESTATE

This chapter covers the tax benefits that the reader can take advantage of when they own and invest in real estate. One way to invest your excess profits is to become involved with real estate. Real estate offers the enticing opportunity to create a recurring cash flow, but are you aware of the tax benefits that come with it?

Deductions

You're able to deduct expenses directly tied to the operation, management, and maintenance of your properties, including:

- Property taxes

The IRS allows you to deduct taxes when the property is primarily used for business purposes.

- Property insurance

Business-related insurance premiums can be deducted; these insurances include:

- Errors and omissions insurance
- Professional malpractice insurance
- General liability insurance
- Workers compensation insurance
- Insurance against fire, storm, theft, accident, and other similar losses
- Mortgage interest

The interest you pay when using a loan to purchase properties can be written off for tax purposes.

- Property management fees

Property management fees are tax-deductible given certain limitations and rules.

- Cost to maintain and repair the building

Repairs that you make to property protect you from future, more expensive improvements, and they are deductible in the year you have made them.

In addition to this, you can write off many expenses you pay to run your real estate investment business. These include:

- Advertisement

Expenses incurred related to the promotion of your business are tax-deductible; these expenses could include:

- Online advertising
- Print advertising
- TV and radio advertising
- Designing and printing business cards, brochures, and business attire.
- Creation of ad copies
- Slogans
- Logos and other graphics
- Website development and social media profile creation
- Seminar and workshop hosting
- Sponsorships
- Office space

Whether it's a home office or a rented office, office space is tax-deductible.

- Building equipment
- Legal and accounting fees

Attorney and accountant fees, as well as property management company fees, can be written off.

- Travel

The cost of traveling to and from your rental properties, for example; gas, and rental costs, could be deducted as business expenses where expenses like airfare, hotel rooms, meals, and team meetings are classified as tax write-offs, especially for investors who invest in properties that are in a different state.

- Note: Running a real estate business means investing through limited partnerships and LLCs.

Depreciation

Depreciation is the process of making slow deductions to the value of an asset over time until such a time as the asset becomes obsolete. Depreciation can be deducted as an expense on your taxes; this ultimately reduces your taxable income because there is no cash flow involved. Depreciation lowers tax liability and helps to recover the cost of enhancements or preservation of the property. The IRS considers specific rules and regulations that control the depreciation and tax deduction claims on these properties. Land cannot be included in the depreciation account when calculating the basis of depreciation as it can only appreciate over time. Depreciation is only subject to the actual assets that can debilitate over time. Deductions stop when an asset becomes aged or is sold out. Depreciation is calculated using the following steps:

- You first need to determine if the property qualifies for depreciation. Some of the crucial criteria to keep in mind are, the investor owns the property, the property should essentially depreciate, the property will be used to generate income.
- Next, calculate the acquisition cost. This could

include installation charges, freight charges, any fees, etc. Land should be excluded from the cost calculations. Any additions or deductions related to the value should account for the costs or income on the property until such a date that it would be made available for rent.

- According to the IRS, you can take the depreciation deduction for the entire expected life of a parcel (27.5 years for residential properties and 39 years for commercial properties).
- Ex. If you purchase a home you intend to rent that is valued at $300,000 (excluding the value of the land it's on), you divide that by 27.5 years. This means you can deduct $10,909 in depreciation each year.
- After calculating the earning potential and the expected expenses for the property, the depreciation value needs to be deducted, which will lower the property's taxable income.

Step-by-Step Example

Let's assume Adam has bought a single-family home in January 2021 for $150,000. In January, he rented it out.

Step 1-Determine the Cost

This cost is determined by the total amount paid for the property. For example, Adam's house was bought for $150,000. The basis is $158,000 when legal and closing costs, as well as financing and due diligence, are added. You now need to deduct the cost of land. In this example, Adam's land is valued at $30,000 (20% of value), and the house is assessed at $120,000 (80% of value). The $30,000 needs to be deducted from the $158,000, which gives Adam a total cost of the house of $128,000. Next, improvements to the property need to be accounted for. Let's say Adam invests $10,000 to get the property ready for rental; then, his basis would be adjusted to $138,000.

Step 2: Determine the Recovery Period

Adam's recovery period will be 27.5 years under the GDS method.

Step 3: Determine the Depreciation Amount

Depreciation equals 3.636% of the adjusted basis depreciated each year. This would mean that Adam's assets would depreciate by $5,018 each year from January 2021. This amount can then be deducted to lower the taxable income.

Depreciation and Cost Segregation

Most real estate uses straight-line depreciation as described previously. This is where the asset or property is depreciated over an allotted amount of time. However, cost segregation creates the opportunity to accelerate depreciation or take advantage of bonus depreciation. With cost segregation, you pay to have a cost segregation study or segregation analysis completed on your property.

By doing this, you'll convert a 1250 property (non-residential real estate property or residential rental property) into 1245 property (tangible personal property):

- Non-residential real properties are subject to a 39-year straight-line depreciation.
- Residential rental properties are subject to a 27.5-year straight-line depreciation.

Converting your property to 1245 can accelerate depreciation on specific components of the property over five, seven, or 15 years.

Benefits of Cost Segregation

Cost segregation reduces taxes and can increase the cash flow of a property quite significantly, especially within the first few years. Personal properties placed into service are eligible for 100% bonus depreciation. This means that investors can deduct 100% of five, seven, and 15 year property within the first year.

Example:

Scenario 1

Maria, who falls within a 24% tax bracket, purchases a 24-unit apartment building for $1,000,000 and places it into service in 2019 but does not utilize a cost segregation study. Her CPA determines the following:

The building is depreciated over 27.5 years, which allows her to take $29,090 as an annual depreciation expense. Her income and expenses were the following:

Maria will have to pay taxes on the $100,000 income that she received from the property. However, the depreciation expense reduces her taxable income and tax liability by

$6,981, and since depreciation is a non-cash expense, Jane will still have $29,090 in cash.

Scenario 2

Maria decides to have a cost segregation study done on her property. The study discovers that the value of the property is broken down as follows:

With the help of the Tax Cuts and Jobs act, Maria can take 100% bonus depreciation on the 5-year property, 7-year property, and 15-year property in the first year. The building will still depreciate over 27.5 years, allowing for an annual depreciation deduction of $20,363. This gives her a depreciation deduction of $260,363 within the first year. Maria will show a loss of $160,363 in the first year. Meaning she will not have to pay any federal or state tax on the $100,000 of net income and can potentially offset other income utilizing the loss. That is equal to $38,487 in tax savings.

Cost Segregation Studies

These studies are carried out by a professional with experience in engineering, architecture, construction, and tax accounting. The purpose is to separate certain qualified items that would typically be considered 1250 property. For example:

- The electrical system
- Specialized kitchen equipment
- Carpeting
- Wallcovering
- Partitions

- A concrete slab floor
- The ventilation system
- Special plumbing
- Lighting features
- The phone system
- The computer system
- Storage tanks

The recovery period (period something can be depreciated) will also be separated from these items. The building itself will still be depreciated over the straight-line depreciation. These studies can cost up to $15,000 but can result in a notable reduction in your tax rate because you can deduct the depreciation values from your taxable income.

How does it work?

Here is how this study is typically conducted:

Conduct a reasonability analysis: This is a complimentary estimate that determines the potential benefits and fees to perform a study for the buildings in question. Your accountant will take time to understand the owner's tax position and the characteristics of the property to ensure a reliable estimate is given concerning the benefits the study could provide.

Gather additional information: Additional information would need to be gathered in this step. Buildings purchased by a taxpayer - the information could include:

- An appraisal
- A property condition report

- An American Land Title Association (ALTA) survey or site map
- The closing purchase documents when the study is done on the acquisition of a property

Constructed or remodeled buildings by a taxpayer, the information includes:

- Overall project costs
- General contractor costs and change order details
- Vendor invoices
- Construction drawings

Analysis: Analyzing the property includes the following:

- Completing an on-site tour of the property
- Examining all drawings and other relevant documents
- Classifying all cost information and estimates, including the personal property within the buildings and land improvements around the property

Complete a report: The completion of a full report is the final step, and this includes:

- Results of the study
- Methodology
- Photos of the property
- Tax law supporting the asset classification

This report should be kept for as long as you own or occupy the property. In case of an audit by tax authorities, this report could provide support for asset classifications.

Capital Gains

Capital gains tax may apply when you sell an asset for a profit. There are two types and each affects your tax differently.

Short-Term Capital Gains

- When you profit from selling an asset within a year of owning it, the gain is counted as regular income.
- If you earn $100,000 from your day job and sell a property for $100,000 profit, you've essentially doubled your taxable income.

Long-Term Capital Gains

- If you've held the asset for a year or longer before selling it, you'll have a significantly lower tax rate than the tax rate on income.
- If your income is low enough, you may not have to pay the tax at all. If you and your spouse file jointly and make a combined $75,000 per year, your long-term capital gains tax rate is 0%. You'll keep every cent of the profit!

Defer Taxes With Incentive Programs

These are special tax codes intended to incentivize investors that you can take advantage of as a property owner.

1031 Exchange

- These were created to reward people who invest their real estate earnings into new deals.
- If the new property you buy is of the same or better value than the one you sell, you can swap them for tax purposes. This allows you to defer paying the capital gains tax on the sale of the first property.
- These exchanges can be used indefinitely, but when you cash out your profits, you'll have to pay any tax owed.

Opportunity Zones

- Opportunity zones are designed by the US Department of Treasury. They are low-income or disadvantaged tracts of land.
- The 2017 Tax Cuts and Jobs Act was intended to encourage investors to put money towards developing and economically stimulating those communities by offering tax breaks.
- You place your unrealized capital gains into a Qualified Opportunity Fund, which goes toward improving the area.
- When following this program, you can reap these rewards: Defer paying capital gains until 2026 (or

until you sell your stake in the fund), increase capital gains by 10% if you hold the fund for five years, 15% for a seven-year period or more. Avoid paying capital gains entirely if you remain invested in the fund for 10+ years.

Self-Employment/FICA Tax

If you have no employer, you become responsible for the entire 15.3% taxes for social security and Medicare. Rental income is taxable as standard income tax but isn't subject to FICA taxes.

Options for Real Estate Investing

What Is Real Estate Investing?

When purchasing a property, you can wait for the property to increase in value so you can gain a huge profit when you sell it, and while you wait, you will be able to rent out the property to generate a monthly income. You can also buy a strip mall and collect monthly rent from hair salons, pizza restaurants, mattress stores, and other businesses. You can even purchase an apartment building with multiple units and collect income from tenants' rentals every month. You would need to conduct as much research as possible to find the right fit for your financial needs.

REITs (Real Estate Investment Trusts)

With a REIT, you invest in real estate without any mainte-nance or management of physical buildings. Instead, you purchase a share of properties owned by a company, similar to investing in a mutual fund (except with real estate instead of stocks). REITs make regular dividend payments to investors. You can also sell your investment for a profit if the value of the REIT goes up. These types of properties often include apartment buildings, hotels, offices, or warehouses. Purchasing shares of these properties are related to investing in mutual funds but with real estate instead of stocks. REITs are usually listed on the stock exchange.

Residential Properties

Investment properties can increase your income significantly, but it may require some work. For this approach, you buy a residential property that you either live in or rent out as you wait for it to appreciate. Renting out the property may allow you to cover all or part of your monthly mortgage payment. This is a more hands-on option unless you choose to outsource to a property management service to handle maintaining and operating properties. One challenge that this option could have is the fact that it could take time to appreciate if it appreciates at all. Researching neighborhoods where properties tend to appreciate could decrease your risk of making a bad investment. Working alongside real estate agents and professionals can help you by showing you historic appreciation numbers for the neighboring properties you are targeting.

Location is very important when considering this option. A house on a quiet street might appreciate quicker in value than a house situated on a busy stretch of road. The same goes for apartment buildings closer to public transport than those located further away. Assigning a property management service is also a good idea when choosing this option because it will take the stress off you for the daily maintenance and operation of the property.

Commercial Properties

Investing in commercial properties is similar to investing in residential real estate. You can purchase an office building and charge companies to rent space, purchase strip malls or retail properties, or even warehouses. The types of commercial properties that you can invest in are office buildings that you can rent out to companies or warehouses that you can rent out to manufacturing companies or retailers for storage purposes. The risks of these properties are the same as with residential properties.

House Flipping

House flipping is often the go-to option for investors who want to generate an income quickly. House flipping involves purchasing a home for a low price, renovating it quickly, and selling it for a profit. Research is key here: You don't want to get stuck with a property that won't sell or that costs more to repair than the profit will cover. You need to work strategically when it comes to restoring the property because you don't want your investment to swallow your profit. Doing the renovation yourself could increase your profits when considering house flipping because you would save a significant amount if you cancel out the use of contractors.

10 Reasons to Invest in Real Estate

Real estate investing can be very lucrative if used correctly.

The most important reasons to invest in real estate are:

- **Steady Cash Flow:** It can increase your monthly income. This doesn't matter if you invest in commercial or residential real estate. You need to be careful to do payment history checks on the tenants you choose to rent your properties out to reduce the likelihood that these tenants will stop their payments.
- **Great Returns:** Properties that increase in value over time can be sold for a profit. Remember that appreciation is not guaranteed, and you would need to invest in the right properties to obtain returns.
- **Long-Term Security:** You can hold onto properties for several years, waiting for the value to appreciate. While you wait for that to happen, you can earn an income from the monthly income from rental checks. Focus on investing for cash flow is the priority here.
- **Tax Advantages:** There are several tax-deductible expenses related to investment properties, including property taxes, mortgage interest, ongoing maintenance, property insurance, property management fees, property insurance, repairs, and the marketing cost related to attracting renters. When you sell your property, the income you receive will not be taxed as ordinary income. Instead, it will be taxed as capital gains, which could mean a lower income tax rate. You will pay even fewer taxes on your capital gains if you invest in properties located in opportunity zones.

- **Diversification:** Real estate could significantly boost your investment diversification, which in turn guards you against economic turmoil. Your investment properties could still be increasing in value even when your other investments like stocks are decreasing, which ensures you don't suffer from too much loss.
- **Passive Income:** Gaining a passive income with as little work as possible sounds great, and this is precisely what property investing does. Rental income is considered passive income.
- **Ability to Leverage Funds:** Leveraging properties means you are using other individuals' money to purchase properties. You can take out either a loan from a bank, mortgage lender or credit union and then pay them back over a certain period. In turn, you can use your rental income to assist in paying back these loans, so you won't need to invest the full amount out of your pocket.
- **Protection Against Inflation:** Real estate investments protect you against inflation. As prices increase on goods and services, so do home values, and rental amounts increase as a result as well. This can provide you with a rising income and appreciation in your property which will protect you financially as other things increase in price.
- **Chance to Build Capital:** You get to build capital with the use of real estate investing. As soon as you sell a property that has appreciated, you boost your capital.
- **Fulfillment and Control:** You become your boss

when you invest in real estate; you also get to make a difference in your community, providing properties to renters or providing businesses with commercial properties that provide services to their communities.

Real Estate Syndications

A commercial real estate syndication is a way that investors can pool their funds together to buy larger, more stable assets than they could have afforded independently. Key terms:

- **Fees:** Some common fees you'll see in a syndication deal include acquisition fee, construction management fee, refinance fee, asset management fee, loan guarantee fee, and/or deposition fee.
- **Syndication Investor:** Also called the limited partners (LPs)
- **Syndication Structures:** There are numerous ways to structure real estate syndications, and this will vary from syndication to syndication.
- **General Partner vs. Limited Partner:** A general partner holds most of the responsibility in syndication. A limited partner usually only contributes money as an investor.
- **506(c) vs. 506(b) Syndication:** The 506(b) offering is for non-accredited investors, while the 506(c) is for accredited investors only.
- **Deal Sponsor:** Also called the syndicator or general partner. Responsible for finding and sourcing

investment opportunities, putting together renovation and operational plans, raising capital, controlling day-to-day responsibilities, and handling investor relations, tax returns, etc.

- **Waterfalls:** Term for the structure that determines how the returns on your investment are distributed to you.

Benefits

You can invest in larger assets and projects which tend to hold their value better and are more liquid than smaller properties. Stability due to higher unit counts/locations:

- Buying a multi-family home versus a single-family home.
- Losing a single renter in a multi-family home is a loss that can be absorbed. Losing a renter in a single-home family home can be devastating if you can't find someone else quickly.

Less money out of your pocket. Completely passive real estate investing and cash flow. Onsite and/or professional management. You won't have to manage the tenants, maintenance, repairs, budgeting, etc.

Vacation Rental Properties

Pros

Earn extra income: Possibly the biggest reason why anyone would want to own a rental property. A vacation property has two major benefits, earning an extra income and having a place where you can break away to. There are a few factors to consider when buying a vacation property:

- Check other listings in the neighborhood you are looking at investing in.
- Look at the nightly rates charged.
- Availability during peak season and off-seasons.

Increase in value: Looking at past and current trends of property values in your preferred neighborhood before purchasing is an important step when considering the purchase of a rental property. Properties in high-demand areas have a greater possibility to increase in value.

Deduction of business-related expenses: Because income is generated from rental properties, it can be classified as a business. Paying taxes on the rental income generated is unavoidable, but business-related expenses can be deducted. These deductions can be anything from house-keeping, restocking, and property management costs. Ensure all receipts are kept for deductions for your tax return filing at the end of the year. Making use of a business credit card could make it easier to keep track of expenses because everything will be in one place.

You will have your own break-away property: Going to your vacation property during the off-season is possibly the best decision you can make. This will increase your revenue because the property will be available for guests during peak season. Having a rental property can give your friends and family a place to break away to as well. A vacation home could be a great idea after retirement should the property be in a desired location.

Cons

Unexpected expenses: There may be times when things need to be fixed in a vacation property, just like a primary residence. As the owner, you would be responsible for any repairs needed for the property. Planning for these costs is important to ensure repairs do not affect your profit. These costs could include utilities, restocking, taxes, and regular maintenance. Dedicating 1% of the property purchase price per year could help you to cover bigger unexpected expenses like a burst pipe or broken air conditioner.

Higher down payment: A vacation home may be considered as a second property, and for that reason, you may be required to pay 20% - 30% on your down payment instead of 3% - 5% you may have on your primary residence. You would also need a higher credit score because you are taking on more debt.

More taxes and fees: Renting out your property for less than 14 days a year could save you from paying taxes on rental income. Renting out your property for more than 14 days a year would mean you need to pay taxes on additional income. Other taxes that are also eligible for payment are state, local, and property taxes. Depending on local tax laws, obtaining a business license and paying sales tax and hotel taxes may also be needed.

Time-consuming upkeep: Regular maintenance and repairs are needed for any property, and with a vacation property, you would need to ensure everything is fine before each new guest. Answering questions and concerns, as well as restocking and housekeeping, could become very time-consuming at times. Traveling costs need to be considered should a vacation home be in a different town or state.

There are two main types of vacation rental properties:

VRBO

VRBO is an acronym for "vacation rentals by owner". This tells you that the vacation property is directly rented out by the owner. Making use of VRBO gives owners the freedom to eliminate management companies. VRBO was started in 1995 and is gaining momentum.

Advantages

Advertising your rental vacation property on VRBO is affordable. The VRBO website and app are relatively easy to navigate on both mobile and laptop devices. Making use of VRBO also simplifies the process of communication, contract signing, and receiving payments. All electronic documents are stored digitally on your VRBO platform, which allows easy access should a guest book your vacation property. You have access to reviews left by clients, which helps with improvements. The filtering option gives guests the opportunity to choose the rental of their choice with their preferences in mind.

Disadvantages

VRBO has introduced a booking service fee that has caused guests to look at other options when booking their vacation rentals. Owners may need to increase their rates to cover the subscription fees that are payable. VRBO also charges a transaction fee when guests book the rental using a credit card. VRBO does not have an option for you to rent out a section on the property. The ability to accommodate two guests on one property is not available. With VRBO, the owner must calculate and pay taxes on the property. Both income and lodging taxes are the sole responsibility of the owner of the property.

AirBnb

Becoming an AirBnb host is an excellent way of earning extra income. But before considering the investment, here are some pros and cons related to this type of investment:

Pros

Cultural experiences: With the variety of visitors from all around the world that you will be hosting, it can only be expected that some exciting stories could be heard. Experiencing the world around you through the experiences of others could give off the feeling of traveling the world from the comfort of your own property.

Flexibility: You can choose when to list your property and how much you want to list it for. You have the ability to remove your listing when you plan to do repairs.

Host protection: AirBnb offers $1 million in protection cover should you be part of their host protection plan. This plan provides protection against damages, theft, and other losses incurred by guests.

Free listing: There are no listing fees applicable to advertising on the website. All you need is high-resolution photos, a great description, location, amenities, and price, and you are good to go.

Return on investment: Purchasing a property in a high-tourism region will have you seeing a return on your investment in no time.

Cons

It's risky: Doing checks on renters is important to ensure that the property is rented to someone trustworthy. Renting a property to an unknown individual could lead to unexpected damages that you, as the owner, would be responsible for.

Landlord and maintenance: Being available at all hours of the day and night come with renting a property. This means that should a guest phone you at 3 am you would need to be available to attend to the emergency.

Legal restrictions: Familiarizing yourself with the laws of the area you are planning to host an AirBnb is very important. Some states may require you to obtain special permits and licenses. You would also need to ensure that the property is completely safe, as injury could lead to possible lawsuits.

7

EXPLORING ENTITIES

This chapter discusses the benefits of using flow-through business entities to get tax breaks. It also covers the differences between LLCs and S-corporations, with pros and cons for each.

Flow-Through or Pass-Through Entities

These entities are legal business entities that pass any income they make directly to the owners, shareholders, or investors. This means that only the individuals are taxed on profits, helping you avoid double taxation, which happens with income from regular corporations.

The Tax Cuts and Jobs Act (TCJA)

This act took effect in 2018 and established a new tax deduction for owners of pass-through businesses. Pass-through owners who qualify can deduct up to 20% of their net business income from their taxes, effectively reducing their income tax rate by 20%. Entities that qualify for this deduction are companies that operate through a pass-through business entity, and examples of these include:

- A sole proprietorship
- A partnership
- An S corporation
- A limited liability company (LLC), or
- A limited liability partnership (LLP)

These types of businesses don't pay taxes themselves, but rather their profits are passed through the business, and the owners then pay the taxes on the money along with their tax returns and their tax rates. Small businesses are often classified as pass-through entities, and over 86% of businesses without employees are sole proprietorships. C corporations do not qualify for these deductions, but they do qualify for 21% corporate tax on all their income.

Qualified Business Income (QBI)

QBI is the income that individuals receive from their pass-through business every year. This is determined by subtracting regular business deductions from the business earnings. This includes rental income as long as this income is classified as business income. Publicly traded partnerships, real estate investment trusts, and qualified cooperatives income can also be included. To qualify, you must have a pass-through/flow-through entity or qualified business income. Income sources that do not qualify for QBI are:

- A short-term or long-term capital gain or loss
- Dividend income
- Interest income
- Wages paid to S corporation shareholders
- Guaranteed payments to partners in partnerships or LLCs members
- Business income earned outside the US

Taxable Income

You need first to figure out what your total taxable income for the year is before you can calculate your pass-through deduction. This would include all your taxable income from all sources minus deductions; this includes standard deductions. Your taxable income needs to be positive to be eligible for the pass-through deduction.

- Note: The deduction cannot be more than 20% of your taxable income.

The QBI is determined for each business, and should you own various that do not qualify as one of these listed below; then you have the option of combining them into one deduction. At least two of the following requirements need to be met to qualify for this deduction:

- The products or services offered by the various businesses can be offered together, or
- The businesses share the centralized business elements like personnel, accounting, legal,

manufacturing, purchasing, human resources, or information technology resources, or

- The businesses are operated together with one or more of the businesses in the combined group.

Should one of these businesses lose income, you will be able to deduct that loss from one of your profitable businesses. That would mean your qualified business loss is zero or less and that you would get no pass-through deductions for the year. The loss will then be carried forward to the next year and is then deducted against your QBI for the relevant year.

Deductions for Income Above the Annual Threshold

Should your income be above the annual threshold ($329,800 if married filing jointly; $164,900 for single filers), your calculations for deductions become more complicated and will then depend on your total earnings and the work that you do. Determine if your business is classified under one of the following service provider categories:

- Health (doctors, dentists, other health fields)
- Legal
- Bookkeeping
- Actuarial science
- Acting
- Consultation services
- Athletes
- Financial related services
- Non-real estate and insurance brokerage services
- Investing and investment management (excluding property managers), or

- Trading and dealing in securities or commodities.

The final categories include businesses where the principal asset is the reputation or skill of one or more of its owners or employees. These are defined by the IRS where a person:

- Receives fees or other income from endorsed products or services
- Licenses her or his images, likeness, name, signature, voice, or trademark
- Receives fees or other earnings for appearing at certain events or on radio, television, or other media forms
- Note: Architecture and engineering services are not included under these personal services. The pass-through deduction is not favored for pass-through owners who provide personal services. They often lose this deduction completely within certain income levels. There are, however, no limitations on pass-through owners who don't provide personal services.

What Are Flow-Through Entities?

The flow-through entity is a device that is commonly used to reduce or avoid double taxation, which usually happens when you have regular corporations. Individuals and businesses are both taxable, which means they are liable to pay taxes on their earnings. Individuals pay income tax, and companies pay corporate tax. However, flow-through corporations avoid paying corporate income tax. The income that a flow-through entity generates is treated as the income of investors, stockholders, or owners. This means that the tax liability that would have been the company's responsibility moves to the individual. Individuals can deduct losses from the company against their income. Flow-through companies are only taxed once on business profits. C corporations are subject to double taxation, first through the corporate tax rate and then when paid out as dividends to shareholders. These entities are commonly grouped into the following:

- Sole Proprietorships: This is a business that is operated by a single person. Income that is generated by such an entity is reported on the individual's tax return. The IRS considers this as a disregarded entity because the revenue is considered the same as the owner's personal income.
- Partnerships (limited, general, and limited liability)
- LLCs: These entities combine flow-through taxation with limited liability. This means the owners or partners are not held personally liable for the company's debt obligation. LLCs often prefer to be taxed as a partnership; this is when the profits/losses are allocated across the LLC owners/shareholders as per the formal ownership agreement, and they are taxed individually.
- S Corporations: Often consists of less than 100 shareholders. They are required to file corporate tax, although profits are often reflected in their personal income taxes.
- Both businesses and individuals are entities that can

be taxed on the money that they earn. You as an individual pay income tax on your wages, while your company pays corporate taxes on its profits.

- When you establish a flow-through entity, the income from the business is treated as the income of the investors, stockholders, or owners:
- These stakeholders pay taxes on business income as if it is personal income and thus pay taxes at their ordinary-income rate.
- Note: The owners can apply losses of the company against their income.

Pros and Cons

Pros

- Regular incorporated businesses pay a flat corporate income tax on profits before distributing them to stockholders and owners. Those shareholders then must report their dividends on their tax returns, essentially taxing the money twice. A pass-through entity allows profit to avoid the initial corporate round tax.
- A pass-through entity protects profits from double taxation. This type of entity is not subject to business taxes.
- In some cases, owners and investors can take extra deductions on their taxes if the business suffers a loss.

Cons

Owners will still be taxed on income that they don't receive:

- Ex: A company takes its profit and reinvests it back into the business rather than distributing it to the owners.
- The owners and investors still need to report their share of the profit and will be taxed on them.

LLCs vs. S Corporations

Choosing the right business structure is key to successfully making the most of your tax incentives.

LLC

A limited liability company. A legal business entity that can be used when forming a business in a more structured and formal way than a sole proprietorship or partnership. An LLC is a type of business entity. Protects the owner from personal liability for any of the debts that a business incurs —typically used by a single owner or a company with two or more owners (partnership)—allowed to have an unlimited number of owners.

Pros

- Personal liability protection
- No double taxation
- Easier to establish and operate than a corporation
- Flexible structure

Cons

- More expensive than a sole proprietorship or partnership
- Must file an annual report that can be hundreds of dollars
- Cannot attract outside investment other than banks

S Corporation

An S corporation is a tax classification rather than a business entity. To become an S corporation, your business must first register as a C corporation or an LLC and meet specific guidelines by the IRS and then make the election to be taxed as an S corporation. These businesses cannot have more than 100 principal shareholders or owners. They cannot be owned by people who are not US citizens or permanent residents or by any corporate entity. They are much more rigidly structured than LLCs:

- Strict regulations for adopting corporate bylaws, conducting annual shareholders meetings, keeping company meeting minutes, stock share regulations.
- They are required to have a board of directors and corporate officers.

Pros

- Provides personal liability protection
- No double taxation
- Can boost credibility with suppliers, creditors, and investors
- Pays dividends to employees

Cons

- Some states may tax S corporations as corporations
- S corporations can incur more fees than an LLC
- S corporations have more regulations and guidelines that must be followed

C Corporation

A C corporation is a legal structure where the owners/shareholders are taxed separately from the entity itself. They are subject to corporate income taxation if dividends are distributed to the owners/shareholders. Owners/shareholders' assets and income are separate from the corporation. This limits the liability of investors and owners since they can only lose the amount they've invested if the business fails.

Corporations pay corporate taxes on all earnings, then distribute the remaining amount to shareholders as dividends. Those individual shareholders must now pay income tax on those dividends. However, they can also reinvest profits in the company at a lower corporate tax rate. Profits that are reinvested in the corporation are not double-taxed.

C corporations are subject to stricter mandates, like holding at least one meeting for shareholders and directors each year. The following need to be kept on record:

- Minutes must be kept for transparency.
- They must keep voting records of the company's

directors and a list of the owners' names and ownership percentages.

- Must have company bylaws on the premises of the primary business location.
- File annual reports, financial disclosure reports, and financial statements.

The Tax Cuts and Jobs Act (TCJA) reduced the corporate tax rate from 35% to a flat 21% with no brackets.

There are many tax advantages linked to a C corporation; some of these include:

Minimizing your overall tax burden: The 2018 tax reform bill was big for C corporations. If a corporation does not regularly make distributions to owners in the form of dividends, then the tax rate of 21% could mean significant tax savings. Salaries taken by business owners are not taxed at a corporate rate; this shifts the tax equation further to their benefit. Businesses who choose not to take dividends and reinvest that amount back into the company may make sense for new or small businesses.

Carrying profits forward and backward: C corporations enjoy flexibility in their determined fiscal year. Shareholders can shift income easily - they can decide what year they want to pay taxes on bonuses as well as when to take their losses. This substantially reduces tax bills.

Accumulation of funds for future expansion: Shareholders can easily shift income readily and retain earnings within the company for future growth; this is usually at a lower cost than that of other pass-through entities.

Writing off salaries and bonuses: C corporation share-holders can serve as salaried employees. Their salaries will still be subject to payroll taxes and Social Security and Medicare contributions; the company may still deduct its share of the payroll taxes. Employees can be paid enough to ensure that no taxable profits remain at the end of the year. Dividends can be taxed twice, and for this reason, share-holders prefer this option.

Medical premium and fringe benefit deductions: When fringe benefits are made available to employees and not just shareholders, then they could have tax write-offs for the C corporation. S corporation shareholders need to declare these benefits as income and then can deduct them from their taxable income on their personal tax return.

Charitable contributions write-off: Charitable contributions can only be written off under a C corporation as a business expense. Deductions over the limit may also be carried over to at least five years in the future.

Carrying losses for years: The IRS does not scrutinize between businesses, and these C corporations could take large capital and operating losses. This is very important for start-up businesses that would like to carry their losses over to future years.

Fewer ownership restrictions: S corporations are not allowed to have more than 100 shareholders and no non-resident or non-individual owners. They may also not issue more than one type of stock. C corporations do not have these restrictions.

Attracting financing: C corporations offer flexible owner-ship in their business structure as well as some form of small business financing that are available to C corporations, like 401 (k) financing. Small businesses can grow as time passes from a small one to a very big one. They may grow big enough to start attracting funding as a publicly traded company on the national stock exchange.

8

MAKING THE MOST OF YOUR STOCKS

This chapter discusses capital gains taxes on stocks and how to maximize them. Generally, any profit you make on the sale of a stock is taxable at either 0%, 15%, or 20% if you've held the shares for more than a year. The dividends you receive from stocks are usually taxable. Capital gains occur when you sell shares of an individual stock, a stock mutual fund, or a stock EFT for more than you originally paid:

- Like with real estate, short-term capital gains apply to stocks that are held for less than one year. These are taxed at your ordinary-income rate.
- Long-term capital gains apply when the shares are held for at least one year.
- Capital gains on stocks are taxed differently than capital gains on a home sale.
- The tax rates of long-term capital gains vary based on filing status and AGI for the year.

Below you will find a table explaining what percentage of tax you will pay depending on your filing status and your capital gains for 2021.

Capital Gains Tax Rate	AGI-Single Filers	AGI-Married Filing Jointly	AGI-Head of Household	AGI-Married Filing Separately
0%	$0-$40,400	$0-$80,800	$0-$54,100	$0-$40,400
15%	$40,401 - $445,850	$80,801 - $501,600	$54,101 - $473,750	$40,401 - $250,800
20%	$445,801 or more	$501,601 or more	$473,751 or more	$250,801 or more

- In addition to those taxes, there is an additional capital gains tax for higher-income investors called the net investment income tax rate:
- This adds 3.8% to the capital gains tax for investors over certain income thresholds
- For 2021, these thresholds are:
- Single/head of household: $200,000
- Married filing jointly: $250,000
- Married filing separately: $125,000

What Assets Are Subject to CGT?

Asset that are subject to Capital Gains Tax are:

- Investment properties
- Shares
- Cryptocurrency
- Business vehicles
- Business/office equipment, and
- Commercial properties

Capital Gains Tax exempt assets are:

- Any assets that were acquired before September 20, 1985
- Your main residence
- Personal vehicles
- Depreciating assets in an investment property

How to Avoid Capital Gains Taxes on Stocks

What Are Capital Gains Taxes?

Capital gains are the profit that you make when you buy low and sell high and are subject to tax. These taxes depend on how long you have had the investment as well as your income level.

It's always a good idea to manage the tax impact when investing in stocks. Tax considerations should form part of the process but should not be the driving force behind your investing decisions. Below are a few ways to minimize or avoid capital gains on stocks:

Work Your Tax Bracket

Capital gains are considered part of your annual gross income (AGI); this could mean that you will move to a higher tax bracket. Once you get close to the upper end of your regular income tax bracket, you might want to consider holding off on selling stocks until a later stage or getting some deduction ready for the current year. This could keep you from being taxed at a higher rate.

Defer Selling Stocks Until a Later Time

What is tax-loss harvesting?

In a nutshell, tax-loss harvesting is selling under-performing stocks to offset the capital gains of an appreciating investment. This strategy is only applicable to non-retirement, taxable accounts. Capital gain is the income you receive when selling investments for a profit. There are two different types of capital gain, and each are taxed differently, namely:

- **Short-Term Capital Gain:** These are gains from investments that you have held onto for less than one year. They are often taxed at your ordinary income tax rate.
- **Long-Term Capital Gain:** These are gains from investments that you have had for more than one year. These often fall under a lower tax rate than short-term gains and will end up at 0%, 15%, or 20%, depending on your income and filing status.

Investors use this tool when selling stocks, mutual funds, EFTs, and other securities that are held in taxable investment accounts at a loss. These losses can be used in various ways, including to offset the impact of capital gains from the sale of these stocks.

Capital gains are used as follows:

- Long-term losses offset long-term gains
- Short-term losses offset short-term gains

Losses from either side are used to offset capital gains first. Alternatively, losses that exceed gains can be used to offset other taxable income up to the amount of $3,000 annually. Losses over that amount can be carried over to future tax years. You need to ensure that you avoid wash sale rules when using a tax-loss harvesting strategy. The rule is that an investor cannot purchase shares of identical or similar security 30 days before or within 30 of selling stocks or other security for a loss. That means there is a 61-day window around the date that you sold your stocks. Misusing this rule could mean that you may not use the tax loss against the capital gains or any other income for that year. The rule is also applicable to the purchase of accounts other than your taxable account, for example, an IRA.

Rebalancing

Rebalancing your portfolio regularly could ensure that your asset allocation stays on its intended path. Should a particular sector or stock have a high-performing year, the rebalance could cause a taxable event. This is not a beginner-friendly strategy, and at some point, reaching out to a tax professional will help you feel more confident in the decisions you make regarding your investments.

Donate Stocks to Charity

There are two benefits related to donating stocks to charity, namely:

- You will not be responsible for the taxes that are incurred on these capital gains as they increase in value.

- You can deduct the value of these shares at the date of donation if you itemize deductions.

Buy and Hold Qualified Small Business Stocks

These stocks are primarily the stocks issued by small businesses that are recognized by the IRS. This is meant to encourage individuals to invest in smaller companies. Between 50% and 100% of the capital gains may be excluded from taxes taken into consideration when they were purchased. This means that according to IRS section 1202, up to $10 million in capital gains could be excluded from your total income.

Reinvest in an Opportunity Fund

Opportunity zones are areas that are economically distressed and offer preferential tax treatment under the Opportunity Act. Capital gains that are reinvested into real estate or business development within opportunity zones can be deferred or reduced from taxes on these reinvested capital gains. Unless the investments are sold before December 31, 2026, the IRS allows the deferral of these gains.

Hold Onto It Until You Die

Holding onto your stocks until the day you die could mean that you would never have to pay any taxes on those capital gains while you live. This could mean that your spouse or dependent who inherits your assets could also be exempt from these taxes because they are able to claim a step-up in the cost basis of inherited stocks. The cost basis of doing this is only the cost of investment, which includes any commissions or transaction fees that you may have incurred. A step-up in basis means that the cost basis will be adjusted to the current value of the investment from the date of the owner's death. This strategy could eliminate some or all the capital gains taxes on an investment that has appreciated in value. Should your beneficiaries decide to sell these highly appreciated stocks, then this will eliminate capital gains and save them a lot of taxes.

Capital gains in your brokerage account after commissions and fees are generally calculated as follows:

capital gains = sale proceeds – cost basis (purchase price of the stock)

The net proceeds in this equation are your capital gains should you decide to sell during your lifetime, and should you choose to defer the stock, then the cost basis is carried over to the new owner. The cost basis is stepped up to the fair market price in the event of death should you die before selling or gifting.

Use Tax-Advantaged Retirement Accounts

Stocks held in an IRA or another tax-advantaged retirement account could result in capital gains from the sale of these stocks to be protected from capital gains taxes in the year the capital gains are realized. These gains will go into the balance of the overall account and will not be subject to taxes until withdrawn in retirement. When certain conditions are met, capital gains that stay in a Roth IRA could be withdrawn tax-free. This is one of the many reasons why many individuals choose to make use of the Roth IRA.

The 10%–12% Tax Bracket

For individuals with a lower tax bracket, the capital gains rate is 0%. In 2021 this has been capped at $40,400 for single filers and $80,800 for joint filers. You need to ensure you follow all the tax rules before you decide to move your stocks over to someone in a lower tax bracket.

9

KEEPING IT TRADITIONAL

This chapter explores the use of traditional retirement plans to defer taxes both temporarily and indefinitely. It covers the two main types of retirement plans and which is the better choice based on current earnings. This chapter will cover the final tax strategy, which is deferring through a traditional retirement plan. While we have explored several different ways to diversify your assets, there's one more thing to cover, and it's something you're probably already familiar with. But there's more you can do than just deferring taxes through traditional accounts: You can turn those temporary tax breaks into permanent tax breaks by taking advantage of the two Ds: debt and death.

Debt

This strategy involves setting up a cash flow that has you borrowing money rather than selling your investments.

When you sell investments, you pay tax. To avoid this, borrow your cash: debt isn't taxable. When you need cash, borrow against your investments instead of selling them. However, this method does cost you money in the form of interest. The interest you incur on mortgage and investment loans may give you a significant tax deduction and reduce the cost of lending and extend your investment portfolio growth. The three main loans that can give you a significant tax deduction are:

- Mortgage Loans

Since the inception of the Tax Cuts and Jobs Act in December 2017, the home mortgage deduction limit has dropped from $1,000,000 to $750,000 for purchases made after December 16, 2017. For one primary and one secondary property, taxpayers may deduct mortgage interest up to the value of $750,000 or $375,000 in the case of a married couple filing separately. This interest may only be deducted should the loan be used for the purchase, construction, or improvement of a qualified property that secures the loan. The IRS defines an improvement as something that adds value to a property, for example, the remodeling of a kitchen, or improvements that could increase the usefulness of a home's life like replacing its roof; this could also include preparing the home for new uses.

- Home Equity Loans

Although rules have changed regarding mortgage interest, there are circumstances where home equity loan interest can still be deducted. Should a home equity loan be used to purchase, build, or improve a taxpayer's primary or secondary property, this interest may be deducted, given the debt does not go over the $750,000 total limit. However, since 2018 taxpayers who have used home equity loans for purposes other than the improvement of properties may not be eligible to deduct this interest.

- Investment Loans

When purchasing taxable investments with the help of an investment loan, then this interest may also be deducted. The amount of interest that a taxpayer will be able to deduct should equal the amount of income that the recognized taxable investment provides for that tax year. A traceable investment portfolio needs to be linked to the investment loan to deduct the income. The taxpayer should also itemize these to claim the deduction preceding the application of standard deduction.

Benefits of an Investment Loan

- Deductible interest is unlimited

When the investment income is the same as the total amount borrowed, then there is no limit to the amount of interest that you can deduct.

- Carried forward deductions

Deductions can be carried forward indefinitely should the interest be more than the investment income.

Considerations of Investment Loans

- Investment Types

The investment that you choose would need to be taxable to qualify for this deduction. For example, an investment that would not be eligible is a tax-exempt municipal bond portfolio.

- Income Types

Interest, dividends, annuity income, and royalties are all examples of income that will qualify for this deduction. You may elect to give up the advantage of a lower tax rate that comes from these income sources to increase the investment income.

- Entity Treatment

There are special rules that apply to limited liability companies, limited partnerships, and operating businesses.

Considerations for a Tax-Efficient Strategy

Example:

Susan is looking at purchasing a $3 million property and having it financed. She must consider the following:

- Option 1: Mortgage Interest Deduction ($750,000)

Susan will only be able to deduct a total amount of $750,000 from the total $3 million of the purchase price to the interest acquired.

- Option 2: Investment Interest Deduction (uncapped)

Should Susan be able to purchase this home using cash, she could borrow up to $1.5 million with the help of the cash-out mortgage and invest the loan in taxable securities. This interest can then be deducted as an investment interest expense, up to the amount of income from the investment. Should the interest paid be more than the investment income, then the interest can be carried over to the following years.

This leads us to the second D:

Death

In many countries, including the US, when you die, your death makes tax deferral permanent. Your family won't be liable for the taxes you owed upon your death.

The two common retirement accounts that enable people to minimize their tax bills are tax-deferred and tax-exempt accounts:

- With a tax-deferred account, tax savings are realized when you contribute to the account. Ex: traditional IRAs and 401(k)s
- With a tax-exempt account, withdrawals are tax-free

in retirement. Ex. Roth IRAs and Roth 401(k)s

- To optimize your tax strategy, you'll want to take advantage of both types of accounts

Tax-Deferred Accounts

These accounts result in immediate tax deductions up to the total amount of your contribution, but when you withdraw from the account, you'll be taxed at your ordinary income. Ex: if your taxable income is $100,000 and you contribute $3,000 to a tax-deferred account, you would pay tax on $97,000. Once you retire, if your taxable income is $80,000, you may choose to withdraw $5,000 from the account. This would bump up your taxable income that year to $85,000. For 2021, you can contribute up to $19,500 to a 401(k) plan, plus a $6,500 catch-up contribution if you are 50 or older. You can contribute a maximum of $6,000 to a traditional IRA, with an additional $1,000 for those 50 and over.

Benefits of Tax-Deferred Accounts

- You'll pay fewer taxes in your current year and may be able to reduce your taxable income to a lower tax bracket if you fall on the threshold.
- When you retire, you'll likely have a lower taxable income and will be in a lower tax bracket even if you withdraw money from the account.
- Tip: For high earners, it's recommended to max out tax-deferred accounts to minimize your current tax burden.
- By receiving an immediate tax advantage, you can

put more money into your account. Say you're paying a 24% tax rate on your income. If you contribute $2,000 to a tax-deferred account, you will receive a tax refund of $480 (0.24 x $2,000) and be able to invest more than the original $2,000, making it compound at a faster rate (assuming you don't owe any taxes). If you do end up owing taxes, the savings will go towards that balance.

Negative Aspects of Tax-Deferred Accounts

- Since the funds that you have contributed to tax-deferred accounts have not been paid out, it is not safe from creditors. This means that should you face bankruptcy; then these funds could still be paid over to creditors.
- With a 401(k) plan, your money could still be intact as opposed to tax-deferred accounts, which are not safe from personal creditors either, should you face bankruptcy. These compensations could be used to pay back any debts that you are owing.
- Tax-deferred accounts are plan-specific which means that the compensations would need to either be left for a few years or until you retire. You will also not be able to take out a loan against these funds even when you are eligible for withdrawals. These rules indicate when and how you are able to withdraw these amounts.
- Some plans give you the opportunity to move the funds from one account to another one while others will not give you this option.

- Some plans will allow you to move funds when you change jobs, while others will not let you do so. Some may also force you to cancel your plan should you terminate your employment, which will significantly impact your tax bill.

Tax-Exempt Accounts

Tax-exempt accounts provide future tax benefits rather than immediate ones. Withdrawals at retirement are not subject to taxes, meaning that your investment will grow tax-free. Ex: if you contribute $1,000 to a tax-exempt account today and receive a yearly 3% return, in 30 years, the account will have $2,427. When you take that money out, you won't owe any taxes on it. In a regular taxable investment portfolio, you would owe capital gains taxes on that growth when you sold the investment. A tax-deferred account would mean you owed ordinary income tax when you took money from that account.

Benefits of Tax-Exempt Accounts

- Taking money out in retirement won't push you into a higher tax bracket. Taxes will only continue to increase in the future, and you'll be able to avoid this with this type of account.
- Note: young adults who are in school or just starting work are ideal candidates for these accounts since they usually have low taxable income and tax brackets compared to what they will have in the future.

- Tax-exempt accounts are an excellent place to invest in highly appreciating assets like cryptocurrency. Using a self-directed individual retirement account (IRA), you can include cryptocurrency and other alternative investments in your retirement portfolio.
- A self-directed IRA is a type of individual retirement account that allows you to use IRA funds to make alternative asset investments.
- Self-directed IRAs have three important components:
- **Custodian:** Holds your IRA and is responsible for the safekeeping and making sure it adheres to IRS and government regulations (in traditional IRAs, these are banks and financial institutions)
- **Exchange:** Manages your cryptocurrency trades. This is where you purchase your cryptocurrency.
- **Secure Storage Solutions:** Protects your cryptocurrency. Most providers of Bitcoin IRAs include proprietary secure storage methods to protect your digital coins.

Bitcoin IRA

A Bitcoin IRA offers an individual higher returns and adds diversity to your retirement portfolio. Keep in mind that cryptocurrency investing is very volatile and risky. Before considering a Bitcoin IRA keep the following in mind.

What Is It?

Also known as a self-directed IRA, allows you to invest in alternative asset classes like real estate, precious metals, and

cryptocurrency. These retirement plans can be both beneficial and risky at the same time; they can enhance your
investment returns and offer a broader diversification.

How Does It Work?

Bitcoin IRAs work on the same principle as a normal IRA,
with the exception that instead of investing in mutual fund
shares, you are investing in cryptocurrency. Their contributions are also limited to $6,000 or $7,000 for individuals over
the age of 50. For self-employed and small business owners,
there are SEP, Simple IRAs, and solo 401(k), which provide
higher contribution limits. You also have the option of
moving funds from a normal IRA to a self-directed IRA.
There are a few differences between a normal IRA and a
self-directed IRA. You may need to be a little more creative
with a Bitcoin IRA. A Bitcoin IRA company might partner
with a particular exchange or allow you to trade using a
third-party crypto exchange.

Advantages

There are several advantages that a Bitcoin IRA offers their
investors, including:

- **Diversification:** Cryptocurrency does not correlate
  with stocks and bonds, and for this reason, they can
  assist in protecting your retirement balance even
  though they may be volatile in their way.
- **High Return Potential:** With volatility comes
  potential high returns. Bitcoin has very high upside
  potential, and for that reason, it is worth the risk,

especially when investing only a small percentage of your overall IRA value.

- **Tax Advantages:** Staying on top of the bookkeeping that comes with cryptocurrency could be a nightmare because you owe taxes every time you sell your cryptocurrency for a profit. When investing in a traditional or Roth IRA, you eliminate this burden because you are not taxed on the money as long as it is in your account. You will also be benefiting from the growth in value that is not lost to taxes.

Disadvantages

- **Fees:** There are more fees involved in investing in self-directed IRAs. These fees could include anything from set-up to trading and account management fees; you need to ensure you are aware of any additional costs linked to cryptocurrency investing for retirement.
- **Exchange Limitations:** There are Bitcoin IRA companies that only work with certain currency exchanges, while others allow you to choose your preferred exchange. Ensure that the company you select will enable you to choose your exchange before investing.
- **Volatility:** Investors who are close to retirement could obtain a substantial risk with a Bitcoin IRA due to its volatility.
- **Capital Losses:** Due to the tax-advantaged status of

a Bitcoin IRA, you are unable to deduct any losses that you may incur when investing.

- **Complexity:** Because a Bitcoin IRA is unable to accommodate assets like stocks, bonds, and mutual funds, they could add complexity to your retirement planning. Therefore, you need to ensure that you have another retirement account along with your Bitcoin IRA to handle moving parts like custodians, exchanges, and secure storage.

Contribution Limits

There are two ways in which you can contribute to your tax-exempt account; these are through a Roth 401 (k) and a Roth IRA. The limitations of these contributions are:

- **Roth 401(k):** $19,500 is the maximum; individuals over the age of 50 may elect to add $6,500 as a catch-up contribution. These limitations are the same with a traditional 401(k) account. Many individuals could benefit from contributions in both a Roth 401(k) and a traditional 401(k) account. You should keep in mind that the total amount paid to both accounts should not exceed either $19,500 or $26,000 for 2021.
- **Roth IRA:** The limitations for this account contribution are $6,000 and $7,000 for individuals over the age of 50.

Many companies offer to match your retirement contribution. Should your company offer this benefit, you would not want to pass up this opportunity. Company matching contributions are considered traditional contributions. Making use of a Roth 401(k) and a traditional plan diversifies the tax status of your retirement savings. You will have access to a taxable and nontaxable account that you can withdraw from whether the taxes increase or decrease.

How to Determine Which Account Is Right for You

This is assuming you can't contribute to both types of accounts. If you have the means to contribute to both, that's your best bet.

Low-Income Earners

You should focus on funding your tax-exempt account over a tax-deferred account. Contributions to a tax-deferred account would provide a minimal current tax benefit with potential large future obligations.

High-Income Earners

Focus on contributing to your tax-deferred account to lower your current marginal tax bracket.

Special Considerations

When taking into consideration the purpose and time frame of your savings, then tax-deferred accounts are preferred as a retirement option since most individuals have minimal earnings and a lower tax rate after retirement. Tax-exempt accounts are most often used for investments as investors realize significant tax-free capital gains.

Tax planning is essential to personal budgeting or investment management decisions. Tax-deferred and tax-exempt accounts are two of the most commonly available options. The only difference between these accounts is when tax is payable.

10

TAX MINIMIZING TIPS FOR SMALL BUSINESSES

T he IRS is exceptionally complex, replete with loopholes, deductions, exemptions, and technicalities that are difficult to understand. Here is a summary of what was discussed in previous chapters, as well as a few extra tips to help you with minimizing your tax burden.

Deferring Receivable Income

You have the power as a small business to decide when you would like to receive income. This means that should you receive income in January 2021; then taxes would need to be paid in April 2022, whereas income received in December 2020 would be payable in April 2021. Sole proprietors, LLCs, and S corporations often use this year-end strategy to minimize their tax bills for the year.

Group Expenses at Year-End

You should always aim to maximize profit and minimize tax. Purchasing supplies at the end of the year could decrease your tax burden. These purchases can include but are not limited to office supplies, prepayment billing, furniture, travel bookings, repairs, and maintenance.

Worn-Out Inventory Write-Offs

If your business is trading in physical products, then it's a good idea to start going through your inventory in December to get rid of any damaged or obsolete goods before year-end. This strategy could significantly increase your business deductions.

Retirement Plan Contributions

Tax-exempt or tax-deferred retirement plans are one of the best ways for small businesses to avoid tax. Retirement plans can significantly, in one way or another, reduce your tax burden, and should you be able to use up your total allowable yearly contribution; you may not be taxed on any of your income.

Auto Expenses

You are allowed to deduct traveling expenses should it be a company requirement for you to travel. There are two ways of doing this:

- **Actual Expense Method:** You would need to document all business-related auto expenses before the deduction can be claimed.
- **Standard Mileage Rate Method:** Deduct a certain

amount for every mile you drive, including tolls and parking charges.

The best method would depend on the business; for example, a newer model vehicle may have a larger deduction when using the actual expense method. You can, however, only deduct business-related activities should your vehicle be used for both business and personal use.

Business-Related Education Write-Off

Going back to college to obtain a degree or attending seminars and training to improve your skills are costs that can be written off on your tax return. Keep in mind that should this education be meant to prepare yourself for another business or a new job; then this may not be deducted as a business-related education deduction. This deduction is only relevant to education that can boost your prospects within current business pursuits.

Travel Expense Deduction

Traveling expenses that are business-related can be deducted. These costs can include airfare, car mileage, taxi service, hotels, food, dry cleaning, and internet services. Should your family accompany you on your business trip, you are only eligible to deduct the costs that are incurred for yourself.

Interest Payment Deduction

Credit or debt financing form a big part of a business's daily running. These costs may be written off in full. This deduction could include costs related to interest, points, fees, and carrying charges that are related to any debt financing that your business may use. This includes personal loans that are used for business purposes. You need to ensure you keep appropriate records when following this strategy. You should have sufficient evidence to prove the debt was used for business.

Charitable Contribution Deduction

Making a charitable contribution at the end of the year is good when you are looking to reduce your upcoming tax bill. Partnerships, LLCs, and S corporations are all eligible to make charitable contributions and still claim the deduction on the shareholder's tax return. C corporations are only eligible to deduct the donation when made from a company contribution. Charitable contributions offer a straightforward way of reducing your tax bill.

Applicable Taxes Write-Off

Day-to-day operation taxes may also be eligible for a write-off. The type of taxes that are involved plays a big part in this deduction strategy. The taxes paid on items that are purchased for your business is deductible as part of the item's cost. The tax incurred on a big business purchase needs to be added to the cost basis of the item and needs to be deducted within the year it was purchased. Taxes incurred on fuel need to be deducted separately. The employer's share of employment taxes can be deducted as a business expense as well. State taxes may be deducted from your company's federal return, and real estate taxes on business properties can be deducted as well.

Advertising Purchases Before Year-End

Business advertising and promotions can be written off at the end of the tax year. This could include an ad in the yellow pages and pay-per-click marketing campaigns, given these costs are correctly documented. Youth sport sponsoring and adorning the side of a car with your business information may also be deducted. Keeping a uniform or photograph of the promotion as proof is a good idea should the IRS decide to audit your tax return.

Legal Expenses Documentation and Deduction

Legal services are considered deductible because they are seen as a necessary service for businesses in different industries. Should you need assistance with incorporation or the drafting of contracts, then your legal bill is a business deduction. To ensure these deductions are not challenged, you would need to save all invoices, bills, and materials relating to your legal bills.

Employ Your Kids

The employment of your children is especially beneficial to small business owners. This is because you can shift a certain amount of the business income to your child and thus lower your tax bracket. The salary that you decide to pay your child will then be taxed at their tax rate.

Stay Clear of an Audit

The IRS has switched its focus from big corporations to smaller businesses like sole proprietors, partnerships, and S corporations. You need to ensure your personal and business expenses are reported separately. Always ensure to report full gross income before any fees, like credit card processing, etc.

Prepaid Expenses Deduction

You will be able to deduct certain prepaid business expenses if the payment covers a period of 12 months or less and if it is ending in the next income year. These payments could include lease payments, interest, rent, business travel, insurances, business subscriptions, etc.

Payroll Tax Software

A third of companies get fined annually for incorrect handling of payroll taxes. Nearly 40% of businesses with employees handle payroll on their own, with the use of paper or spreadsheets. Payroll tax software can help you automatically calculate, deposit, and file taxes for yourself.

Get Organized

The perfect way to get organized is by setting up a filing system that could help you keep track of your paperwork and keep everything in one place. Separating your documents into a monthly category can help you determine what needs to be filed. You might also want to reconcile your bank account at least once a month to ensure that all your accounts are matching up with your receipts.

Early Tax Bird

You can save a lot of tax money if you file your tax returns early. You could incur penalties should you fail to file your tax return on time as well as pay your taxes on time. Penalties can be up to 5% of your unpaid taxes each month, going up to 25%. You should still file your tax return even if you are unable to pay your tax bill. By doing this, you will avoid the failure to file a penalty.

Pay Estimated Taxes

You can make provision to pay an estimated tax amount throughout the year; this will help you to avoid interest and penalties. There are many small business owners that are unable to pay their tax bills because they didn't put money towards it and are then charged interest and penalties. You should ensure to always keep enough funds aside for taxes.

Keep Up With Tax Laws

Throughout the year, the tax law changes with major legislation, court cases, and IRS appearances. These could present positive tax opportunities, and should you be aware of them, you can start acting on them immediately.

Year-End Bill Payments

Make sure to pay all outstanding bills that may be due in January at the end of December. This could reduce your tax burden in April.

Penalty Relief Advantage

Penalties that can qualify for relief are penalties incurred for failing to file a tax return or paying on time. Individuals who can apply for this relief are those who follow the legal requirements but fail to meet them due to unforeseen circumstances or individuals who are able to resolve the penalty notice issue.

Employ Family Members

The government usually favors Family-owned businesses. One thing you need to keep in mind, especially when employing children, is that you need to follow child labor laws and ensure you are paying reasonable rates. You should also ensure that this will work to the benefit of your company to qualify for this exemption.

Hire Independent Contractors

By making use of independent contractors, you are exempt from paying payroll taxes as well as providing other benefits. Should your independent contractor be classified as an employee, you could incur penalties, so be sure you understand the difference between employees and contractors. You may want to consult a tax professional before classifying someone as an independent contractor.

Start a Retirement Plan

Retirement plans hold a lot of advantages when it comes to tax deductions. Your employees, your business, and yourself can gain several tax benefits from a retirement plan. You can attract and retain more qualified employees should they know that you provide a retirement plan. Retirement plans need to be open by the 31st of December to qualify for the current year.

Change Business Structure

Your business structure could have an impact on your taxes. Sole proprietorships, partnerships, and S Corporations are taxed at your ordinary tax rate, while shareholders of a C corporation are taxed at corporate rates and are taxed again when they report distributions on their tax returns. You may have to change your business structure should you not be able to take advantage of certain deductions.

Make Smart Investment and Purchases

Timing your purchases and investment is crucial as they can affect your tax liability for the current or next year. Purchasing equipment before the end of the year could give you a tax deduction in the current year; the same goes for services.

What Should Be Taxed and What Not

Income generated from the sale of business goods or services are taxable. However, some cash increases aren't taxable; these include bank loans, lines of credit, and loans from the business owner.

Auto Expense Deduction Advantages

When a vehicle is used for business purposes, you can deduct these expenses. This is a good strategy for businesses to save on their taxes. You can deduct expenses like gas, repairs, and insurance. You would need to calculate the percentage of personal use to business use should you only have one vehicle for both. If you drive 15,000 miles per month and your mileage tracker shows that 6,000 of those were business-related, then you would divide 6,000/15,000, which would bring you to 40%. That 40% would then be the total car expenses that can be used as a business deduction.

Separate Business and Personal Accounts

Ensuring that you have a separate checking account and credit card account for your business is very important. This will make the process of organizing and managing your books a lot easier when it comes to tax season. You would need to provide any documentation that supports legitimate business expenses should the IRS come knocking for an audit.

Electronically Sending Tax Returns

Sending your tax returns electronically could give you the peace of mind that it is received on time. There are many software programs available that will allow you to e-file tax returns. With E-filing, you will receive a confirmation number as soon as your tax return has been received by the IRS. Should you expect a return then with an electronic tax return, it should be processed much faster. If you use a CPA or other tax professional, they will e-file your tax return as well.

Check Your Tax Return Carefully

Should you use the service of a CPA or other tax professional, then you need to make sure that everything is in order before signing. The moment you sign the document, you agree 100% that everything is reported by your business. You will be held responsible by the IRS should something be incorrect.

IRS Video Portal

To stay on top of tax code changes that could save you money, you might want to have a look at the IRS video portal dedicated to small businesses. There are videos available to entrepreneurs to assist with the starting and running of a business legally and tips on how to take advantage of tax deductions.

Using a Tax Professional

Making use of a CPA or other tax professional could be advisable in certain situations, and fortunately, they are quite affordable. Tax professionals are well versed in the most favorable tax deductions and credits and would know exactly what to do to save the taxpayer money with their taxes. A good CPA will save you more in taxes than their fees.

Unused Inventory Donations

Donating unused inventory to charity organizations could help to reduce your tax. You can also save money because you would not need to store them. Money, supplies, and property donations are considered as deductible expenses. By making local contributions, you establish yourself as a caring member of the community.

Medical and Charitable Miles Deduction

Miles driven for business purposes are not the only ones that can be deducted. Miles driven for medical purposes as well as for charitable purposes can all be deducted. Make sure that you calculate these properly to ensure you can use them when you file your return.

Take the Home Office Deduction

Many small businesses are unaware that setting up a home-based business could give them a tax deduction. Make a note of everything in relation to the way your business is run, and then report it to your CPA. You would need to include everything to ensure that you don't miss out on something that could give you a tax deduction.

Defer Your Income

You may consider invoicing a customer in January for a big project done in December to reduce your taxable income, but you would also need to keep in consideration your client's budget and tax strategy.

Fully Deductible Business Expenses Advantages

Business expenses can be deducted directly from gross income. Ordinary and necessary expenses for the daily running of your business can be deducted.

College Education Expense Write-Off

Employing your college-going children and adding them to your payroll for performing business-related tasks could mean that you pay that child a certain amount a year. That amount cancels the child's own standard deduction. Your child will, in return, be able to save for or pay for their own college education with the use of the deductible wages you pay, and there are no payroll taxes for individuals under 18 years old if appropriately structured.

Deduct Phone, Internet Service, and Utility Bills

Phone calls, internet services, and utilities are tax-deductible business expenses should they only be utilized for business purposes, and there is valid documentation to prove it. If not strictly for business purposes, a pro-rata portion can be deducted. The interest incurred on a business credit card as well as the annual fees are also tax-deductible business expenses.

Tax Breaks When Selling Appreciated Assets

Gifting actual stock assets to a child or family member with a lower tax bracket could save you a lot on your taxes. You may also contribute stock to a charity, and by doing this, neither you nor the organization will be liable for capital gains taxes.

Add Employee Benefits Instead of Giving Raises

Increasing your contributions to employee health insurance with the same amount as a salary increase could benefit your employees and save on taxes for your business. Benefits given to employees eliminate certain taxes than would have come up if the employee were to get a raise.

Look for Carryovers

There are certain credits and deductions that have set limits that could prevent you from using them in full for the current year but would allow you to carry them over to the following years. These include capital losses, charitable contribution deductions, general business credits, home office deductions, net operating losses, etc.

Tax, Legal, and Educational Expenses Advantages

Fees paid to accountants, lawyers, or business consultants are considered business expenses and directly related to the daily operation of your business. They can also be deducted from your taxes in the year that they are paid.

Small Business Tax Credits Advantages

Apply for every tax credit that you are eligible for. These are usually offered by the IRS to motivate businesses to complete certain activities. They directly reduce your tax burden, whereas tax deductions reduce the amount of your taxable income. You can visit the IRS website to find out what credits you have available for your business.

CONCLUSION

"The only difference between a tax man and a taxidermist is that the taxidermist at least leaves the skin."

— MARK TWAIN (1835–1910)

Tax can be a very difficult thing to understand. Throughout this book, I have talked about various aspects of tax planning and how it can be used to your benefit. I hope that you have found this book informative and helpful. Some of the key takeaways that I hope you start implementing in your business practices are:

- Understanding the difference between a tax deduction and tax credit
- Knowing when to itemize and when to take the standard deduction
- How long do you need to hold onto your tax records

- Understanding the four categories of the cashflow quadrant
- Reaching financial freedom with the use of asset classes
- Balancing your portfolio
- Realizing what deductions you can qualify for
- How to shift income to lower your taxes
- Most important small-business tax credits
- Understanding the benefits of real estate
- Knowing which entity type is the best for your business
- Optimizing your stocks and deferring capital gains taxes
- Retirement planning and what options are available

"I am proud to be paying taxes in the United States. But I would be just as proud to pay half of the money."

— ARTHUR GODFREY

Reaching financial freedom by minimizing your taxes is possible, and if you follow the information provided in this book, you will be sure to achieve it. The world needs more female entrepreneurs that can boost our economy, and with this book, I hope to have motivated more ladies to continue to achieve this. Getting discouraged by tax credits and deductions is completely normal but understanding them is not as difficult. Running a business is a challenging task but a very doable one.

Everyone wants to build wealth and leave a legacy for their family. And with this book, I hope to have reinforced that dream.

If you have found this book to be informative and helpful, I would love to hear from you. Now that you understand the ins and outs of tax incentives, it's time to start making the most of it! Take this opportunity to assess your own business and find where you can start saving money and maximizing your returns.

If you need help or want to schedule a Free 60-minute Tax Assessment with me, there is a link and QR Code on the next page.

Please leave a review and rating on this book. I love to hear from every single reader, and your feedback is appreciated because it gives me the motivation to keep motivating you.

LEAVE A 1-CLICK REVIEW

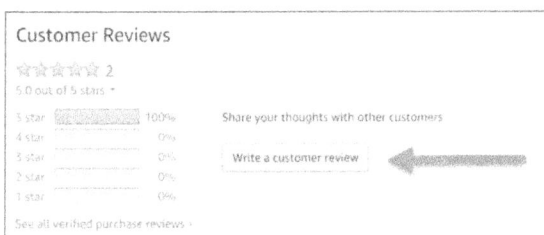

I would be incredibly <u>thankful</u> if you could take just 60 seconds to write a brief review on Amazon, even if its just a few sentences!

FREE

1-HOUR TAX ASSESSMENT

We'll walk through...
-Which deductions you should be
taking.
-The legal entity structure most CPA's
don't recommend.
-The 2 retirement strategies even solid
financial advisors miss.

A Free Gift to Our Readers
Visit the link or QR code below to schedule your
FREE 1-hour tax assessment
www.amzaccountingsolutions.com/tax-planning-book

REFERENCES

5 main types of assets – ALL about CELSIUS. (n.d.). All about Celcius. allaboutcelsius.com/5-main-types-of-asset-classes/

Adams, Hayden. (2021, September 28). *How to cut your tax bill with tax-loss harvesting.* Schwab Brokerage. www.schwab.com/resource-center/insights/content/reap-benefits-tax-loss-harvesting-to-lower-your-tax-bill

Bell, K. (2021, June 16). *How long should you keep tax records?* NerdWallet. www.nerdwallet.com/article/taxes/how-long-to-keep-tax-records

Berry-Johnson, Janet. (2021, February 22). *Your complete guide to 2021 U.S. small business tax credits | FreshBooks Blog.* FreshBooks Blog - Resources & Advice for Small Business Owners. www.freshbooks.com/blog/8-tax-credits-every-small-business-owner-should-know-about

Bird, Beverley. (2021, November 26). *What is income shifting?* The Balance. www.thebalance.com/what-is-income-shifting-5201145

Burggrabe, Roger. (2021, August 9). *Get answers to FAQs about cost segregation studies.* Moss Adams. www.mossadams.com/articles/2021/08/cost-segregation-faqs

Business tax credits | Internal Revenue Service. (n.d.). IRS. www.irs.gov/businesses/small-businesses-self-employed/business-tax-credits

Byrne, Steve. (2021, May 24). *Council post: Exploring the tax benefits of real estate investing.* Forbes. www.forbes.com/sites/forbesbusinesscouncil/2021/05/24/exploring-the-tax-benefits-of-real-estate-investing/

Carson, Chad. (2020, August 23). *The cashflow quadrant explained - How you earn income matters.* Coach Carson. www.coachcarson.com/cash-flow-quadrant-how-earn-matters/

Chang, Ellen. (2021, March 12). *12 common deductions you can write off on your taxes.* Forbes Advisor. www.forbes.com/advisor/taxes/12-common-deductions-you-can-write-off-on-your-taxes/

Cothern, Lance. (2018, December 18). *How to balance your portfolio — Using businesses, commodities, paper assets, & real estate - WealthFit.* Wealth Fit. wealthfit.com/articles/balance-your-portfolio/

El-Sibaie, Amir. (2021, November 10). *Federal tax rates & brackets*. Tax Foundation. taxfoundation.org/publications/federal-tax-rates-and-tax-brackets/

Esajian, JD. (2021, November 8). *The best tax benefits of real estate investing*. FortuneBuilders. www.fortunebuilders.com/real-estate-investing-tax-benefits/

Financial, IRA. (2019, January 1). *What is a self-directed IRA LLC?* IRA Financial Group. www.irafinancialgroup.com/learn-more/self-directed-ira/what-is-a-self-directed-ira-llc/

Fishman, Stephen. (2021). *Rules for deducting prepaid business expenses*. Nolo. www.nolo.com/legal-encyclopedia/rules-deducting-prepaid-business-expenses.html

---. (2021). *The 20% pass-through tax deduction for business owners*. Nolo. www.nolo.com/legal-encyclopedia/the-new-pass-through-tax-deduction.html.

Frankle, Neil. (2012, July 12). *How to use income shifting to save taxes*. Wealth Pilgrim. wealthpilgrim.com/use-income-shifting-to-lower-your-taxes/

Ganti, Akhilesh. (2019). *Asset class definition*. Investopedia. www.investopedia.com/terms/a/assetclasses.asp

Gariepy, Laura. (2021, November 19). *Top 6 tax benefits of real estate investing*. Rocket Mortgage. www.rocketmortgage.com/learn/tax-benefits-of-real-estate-investing

Guidant. (2018, June 6). *10 tax advantages of c corporations for small businesses.* Guidant Financial. www.guidantfinancial.com/blog/10-tax-benefits-of-c-corporations/

Hall, Brandon. (2021, December 30). *Cost segregation: The strategy real estate investors use to pay little to no taxes on their investments.* The Real Estate CPA. www.therealestatecpa.com/blog/costsegregation

Hayes, Adam. (2021, July 3). *Flow-through entities: What you need to know.* Investopedia. www.investopedia.com/terms/f/flow-through.asp

Home office expenses: What you need to know. (2020, November 24). Wagenmaker & Oberly, LLC. wagenmakerlaw.com/blog/home-office-expenses-what-you-need-know

Imber, Jonathan. (2021, June 3). *Is deferring taxes the best thing for your retirement savings?* Kiplinger. www.kiplinger.com/taxes/tax-planning/602893/is-deferring-taxes-the-best-thing-for-your-retirement-savings

Is c corporation your best option under the new tax law? (n.d.). Frazier & Deeter, LLC. www.frazierdeeter.com/insights/is-c-corporation-your-best-option-under-new-tax-law/

Johnson, Jamie. (2021, November 18). *How to flip a house: A starting guide.* Rocket Mortgage. www.rocketmortgage.com/learn/how-to-flip-a-house

Kagan, Julia. (2019). *How c corporations work.* Investopedia. www.investopedia.com/terms/c/c-corporation.asp

---. (2021, July 20). *Uniform transfers to minors act (UTMA).* Investopedia. www.investopedia.com/terms/u/utma.asp

Kenton, Will. (2021, November 23). *Do you qualify for the child and dependent care tax credit?* Investopedia. www.investopedia.com/terms/c/childanddependentcarecredit.asp

---. (2021, April 18). *Family limited partnership (FLP).* Investopedia. www.investopedia.com/terms/f/familylimitedpartnership.asp

Kerr, Micheal. (n.d.). *Tax benefits of an s corp.* Small Business - Chron.com. smallbusiness.chron.com/tax-benefits-s-corp-4183.html

Kiyosaki, Kim. (2013, May 9). *Which asset class is right for you?* Rich Dad | Financial Education & Coaching for Everyone. www.richdad.com/asset-class

Kiyosaki, Robert. (2011, June 14). *Rich dad fundamentals: The cashflow quadrant.* Rich Dad | Financial Education & Coaching for Everyone. www.richdad.com/cashflow-quadrant

LLC | Internal Revenue Service. (n.d.). IRS. www.irs.gov/credits-deductions/individuals/llc

M.D, Passive Income. (2017, November 15). *Why doctors need to understand the cashflow quadrant.* Passive Income M.D. passiveincomemd.com/doctors-need-understand-cashflow-quadrant/

Majaski, Christina. (2021, April 10). *LLC vs. S corporation: What's the difference?* Investopedia. www.investopedia.-

com/articles/personal-finance/011216/s-corp-vs-llc-which-should-i-choose.asp

McIntyre, Georgia. (2021, February 5). *21 small-business tax deductions you need to know.* NerdWallet. www.nerdwallet.com/article/small-business/small-business-tax-deductions-guide

McNeil, Andre. (2021, April 22). *How to get the most money back on your tax return.* Investopedia. www.investopedia.com/financial-edge/0312/how-to-get-the-most-money-back-on-your-tax-return.aspx

Miner, Josh. (2020, December 15). *Tax treatment for employee medical expense reimbursement.* People Keep. www.people-keep.com/blog/tax-treatment-for-employee-medical-expense-reimbursement

Napoletano, E. (2021, June 30). *Bitcoin IRA: How to invest for retirement with cryptocurrency.* Forbes Advisor. www.forbes.com/advisor/retirement/bitcoin-ira/

Opportunity zones | Internal Revenue Service. (n.d.). IRS. www.irs.gov/credits-deductions/businesses/opportunity-zones

Orem, Tina. (2021, June 16). *Tax planning for beginners: 6 tax strategies & concepts.* NerdWallet. www.nerdwallet.com/article/taxes/tax-planning

---. (2021, April 12). *Taxes on stocks: What you have to pay, how to pay less.* NerdWallet. www.nerdwallet.com/article/taxes/taxes-on-stocks

Pinkasovitch, Arthur. (2021, April 11). *Retirement savings: Tax-Deferred or tax-exempt?* Investopedia. www.investopedia.com/articles/taxes/11/tax-deferred-tax-exempt.asp

PNC. (2021, April 14). *Tax efficient borrowing strategies.* PNC. www.pnc.com/insights/wealth-management/markets-economy/tax-efficient-borrowing-strategies.html

Prakash, Priyanka. (2021, October 14). *Small-business tax credit: The complete guide.* NerdWallet. www.nerdwallet.com/article/small-business/small-business-tax-credits-guide

Rae, David. (2021, March 4). *The 19 most valuable tax deductions for your small business.* Forbes. www.forbes.com/sites/davidrae/2021/03/04/the-19-most-valuable-tax-deductions-for-your-small-business/?sh=7442802344eb

---. (2018, November 13). *What is the best business entity to pay the least taxes?* Forbes. www.forbes.com/sites/davidrae/2018/11/13/business-entity-to-pay-the-least-taxes/?sh=29dd32fe1123

Rafter, Dan. (2021, June 26). *Why invest in real estate? 10 benefits.* Rocket Mortgage. www.rocketmortgage.com/learn/benefits-of-real-estate-investing

Raskulinecz, Jaime. (2021, March 16). *Council post: How to invest in cryptocurrency with a self-directed IRA.* Forbes. www.forbes.com/sites/forbesfinancecouncil/2021/03/16/how-to-invest-in-cryptocurrency-with-a-self-directed-ira/

Real estate syndication: How it works and how to participate. (2021, April 8). Financial Samurai. www.financialsamurai.-

com/real-estate-syndication-how-it-works-and-how-to-participate/

Realized capital gains | Vanguard. (n.d.). Investor Vanguard, investor.vanguard.com/investing/taxes/realized-capital-gains#:~:text=Capital%20gains%20are%20profits%20on

Reinicke, Carmen. (2021, August 17). *Stock trading could mean a hefty tax bill next year. What you need to know.* CNBC. www.cnbc.com/2021/08/17/stock-trading-could-mean-a-hefty-tax-bill-what-you-need-to-know.html

Retirement savings contributions savers credit | Internal Revenue Service. (n.d.). IRS. www.irs.gov/retirement-plans/plan-partic-ipant-employee/retirement-savings-contributions-savers-credit

Sharma, Rakesh. (2019). *Pros and cons of investing in bitcoin IRAs.* Investopedia. www.investopedia.com/tech/pros-and-cons-investing-bitcoin-iras/

Solutions, Ramsey. (2021, September 21). *15 small-business tax deductions.* Ramsey Solutions. www.ramseysolutions.com/taxes/small-business-tax-deductions

Tweddale, Alaina. (2020, November 2). *How tax-loss harvesting can turn investment losses into wins.* FinanceBuzz. financebuzz.com/tax-loss-harvesting

Wohlner, Roger. (2021, May 5). *How to avoid capital gains tax on stocks (7 tricks you need to know).* FinanceBuzz. financebuzz.com/how-to-avoid-capital-gains-tax-on-stocks